More Praise for *Strategic Analytics*

"Levenson breaks analysis down into a st[illegible] how to capture data and truly implement analytics in organizations, creating capabilities that drive strategy execution and, ultimately, competitive advantage. A must-read for HR professionals who want to build strategic partnerships and drive game-changing results."

—Mike Johnson, Chief Human Resources Officer, UPS

"Informed business and HR leaders know how important it is to connect business and talent outcomes. They appreciate the need for art and science but rarely have the methodology or tools to make the science real. *Strategic Analytics* helps solve this problem, providing insight on applying big data and analytics to unlock value for leaders and for organizations."

—Scott Pitasky, Executive Vice President and Chief Partner Resource Officer, Starbucks

"*Strategic Analytics* addresses one of the key complaints about HR today—that the function is not aligned with driving the business strategy. Levenson gives a step-by-step approach for leveraging analytics to identify the right levers to drive business strategy and organizational effectiveness. The book is both comprehensive and pragmatic, with thoughtful examples to help HR and business leaders alike."

—Tracy Faber, Senior Vice President, Human Resources, McKesson

"A real breakthrough. *Strategic Analytics* is a must-read for line and human resource executives who strive to make their organization and human resource system a source of strategic advantage. The systemic framework for rigorous diagnosis of organization alignment problems will help executives avoid simple but wrong responses that undermine effective strategy execution."

—Michael Beer, Professor Emeritus, Harvard Business School, and cofounder of TruePoint

"Levenson offers a highly useful framework for sharpening the focus of analytics within large, complex organizations. This book cuts through much of the hype surrounding the topic with a pragmatic review of methods that will generate actionable insights within an enterprise. *Strategic Analytics* should redirect efforts that often generate large quantities of data without really impacting business results."

—Alan May, Executive Vice President, Human Resources, Hewlett Packard Enterprise

"Do you ever feel like you have all the data in the world but still don't know how to use it or you're not sure which analytics to use? So many practitioners don't solve their organizational issues because analytics without strategy are useless, or their strategies aren't aligned organizationally so the analytics don't matter. In this essential book, Levenson provides meaningful, actionable insights for business leaders and HR practitioners to align strategies and priorities to improve organizational effectiveness and drive bottom-line results."

—Kim Warmbier, Executive Vice President, Human Resources, Dean Foods

"*Strategic Analytics* is the book we have been waiting for. Levenson provides a road map to analyze performance gaps in strategy execution and the causal linkage with how the organization is designed and managed. He shows the role high-performance work design plays in strategy execution, which is the key design area in the new digital modern organization. This book puts all the pieces together to provide a clear analytic approach to improve organizational effectiveness."

—Stu Winby, CEO, SPRING Network

"Getting people and practices aligned to achieve strategy is one of the biggest stumbling blocks in modern management, often made worse by conflicting messages coming from workplace metrics and overall business metrics. *Strategic Analytics* offers practical advice on how to straighten out those different measures. New and much-needed guidance for getting strategy execution right."

—Peter Cappelli, Director, Center for Human Resources, Wharton School of Business

"*Strategic Analytics* is a great road map for the journey from big data and big confusion to focused and practical sense—making sense through better business insights. Levenson provides a user-friendly approach for what to analyze, why to analyze it, and how to make more powerful business decisions as a result."

—Ian Ziskin, President, EXec EXcel Group LLC, and former Chief Human Resources Officer, Northrop Grumman

"Levenson nails the essence of successful analytics work with the statement that 'effective analytics is a team sport.' Up to now, analysis in organizations has been a suboptimized, multiheaded monster with each head eating alone. *Strategic Analytics* shows how to effectively use a holistic integrated approach."

—Jac Fitz-enz, CEO Human Capital Source

STRATEGIC ANALYTICS

STRATEGIC ANALYTICS

ADVANCING STRATEGY EXECUTION AND ORGANIZATIONAL EFFECTIVENESS

ALEC LEVENSON

Berrett–Koehler Publishers, Inc.
a BK Business book

Berrett-Koehler Publishers, Inc.
1333 Broadway, Suite 1000
Oakland, CA 94612-1921
Tel: (510) 817-2277 Fax: (510) 817-2278 www.bkconnection.com

Ordering Information
Quantity sales. Special discounts are available on quantity purchases by corporations, associations, and others. For details, contact the "Special Sales Department" at the Berrett-Koehler address above.
Individual sales. Berrett-Koehler publications are available through most bookstores. They can also be ordered directly from Berrett-Koehler: Tel: (800) 929-2929; Fax: (802) 864-7626; www.bkconnection.com
Orders for college textbook/course adoption use. Please contact Berrett-Koehler: Tel: (800) 929-2929; Fax: (802) 864-7626.
Orders by U.S. trade bookstores and wholesalers. Please contact Ingram Publisher Services, Tel: (800) 509-4887; Fax: (800) 838-1149; E-mail: customer.service@ingrampublisherservices.com; or visit www.ingrampublisherservices.com/Ordering for details about electronic ordering.

Printed in the United States of America

Berrett-Koehler books are printed on long-lasting acid-free paper. When it is available, we choose paper that has been manufactured by environmentally responsible processes. These may include using trees grown in sustainable forests, incorporating recycled paper, minimizing chlorine in bleaching, or recycling the energy produced at the paper mill.

Library of Congress Cataloging-in-Publication Data

Levenson, Alec Robert, 1966-
Strategic analytics : advancing strategy execution and organizational effectiveness / Alec Levenson.
pages cm
Includes bibliographical references.
ISBN 978-1-62656-055-0 (pbk.)
1. Strategic planning. 2. Management--Statistical methods. 3. Decision making. 4. Organizational effectiveness. 5. Personnel management. I. Title.
HD30.28.L467 2015
658.4'012--dc23

2015021656

First Edition
20 19 18 17 16 15 10 9 8 7 6 5 4 3 2 1

Full-service book production: Adept Content Solutions; Urbana, IL

Cover Design: Steven Pisano

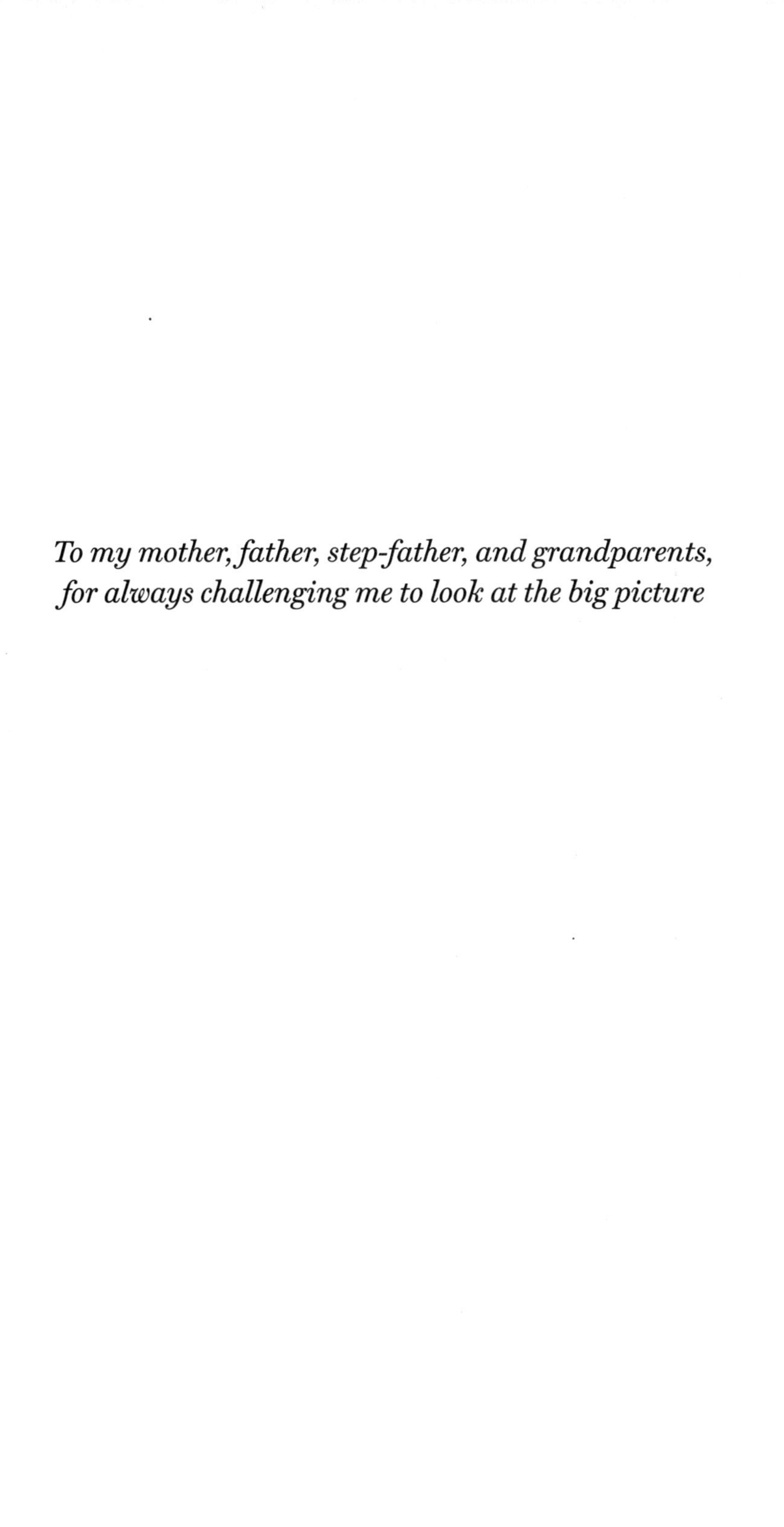

To my mother, father, step-father, and grandparents,
for always challenging me to look at the big picture

Contents

List of Figures and Tables

Preface

Most organizations today have mountains of data they use to understand organization processes and customer behavior. Yet the insights the data provide haven't made organizations themselves more effective. A primary reason is that human resources (HR) and those running the business do not share common approaches or analytical frameworks for identifying critical issues and setting priorities. As a result they often talk past each other. Business leaders are not held accountable for decisions about employees and treat them almost like an afterthought. For HR leaders, essential business outcomes are not exactly an afterthought, but often close to it.

Over its more than thirty-five-year history, the Center for Effective Organizations (CEO) in the Marshall School of Business at the University of Southern California has worked to bridge the gap between research and practice, guided by a careful balance of scientific rigor and pragmatism. During this time there has been a revolution in the tools and information available to us and to our partnering organizations.

Even with all of this information, we find that organizations struggle as much as ever to achieve strategic objectives and improve organizational effectiveness. The purpose of this book is to help decision makers at all organizational levels, in both the business and HR, use analytics more effectively to achieve their goals. The frameworks and advice will help you break out of the traditional mode of uncoordinated analytics and decision making. Applying the tools and lessons provided here should lead to both improved execution of your strategy and increased effectiveness of your organization—if you have the determination and perseverance to develop a plan consistent with this approach and stick with it.

Introduction

Integrating Enterprise and Human Capital Analytics

"The vast majority of strategic initiatives never succeed." "Organizations fail not because they have the wrong strategy but because they do not execute the strategy properly."

Statements like these have been repeated so often they have become conventional wisdom. An entire industry of management consultants exists to help companies define the right strategy so that they won't fail. Yet failure, or at least muddling through, is still much, much more common than outright success (Worley, Williams, and Lawler, 2014).

This book is about how to use analysis to improve both strategy execution and organizational effectiveness, including the investment decisions made through the annual budgeting process. The book does not provide one-size-fits-all solutions like strategy maps, balanced scorecards, the "right" leadership behaviors, communication strategies, or any of the numerous other solutions that are supposed to fix what ails all organizations.

The focus here is on *analysis*. If you want a deeper understanding of *why* the execution of your strategy falls short because of issues with the structure and processes of your organization, then this is the book for you. Through analysis you can determine where execution works well and where it does not. With that information you can evaluate the solutions, determine which one(s) to implement, and channel incremental budget dollars where they will best support the strategy. If you are looking for a quick-fix solution, look somewhere else.

The book addresses a large gap that exists today in how organizations conduct analytics. On the one hand, we have at our fingertips access to the most powerful computers, the largest databases on organizational processes, and ever-expanding information on consumer behavior and the way commerce is conducted worldwide. On the other hand, organizations struggle as much as ever to achieve strategic objectives and improve organizational effectiveness. We need something different.

The power and danger of simplification. Organizations are complex places. There are tons of moving parts that have to be aligned and work well together to produce the products and services for the customers. Cognitively, people have a hard time focusing on too many things at once. We make their job objectives as simple as possible so they can focus their energy productively. If we didn't do this, people easily could get lost figuring out what they should be doing.

A primary vehicle for reduced complexity is standard business processes—specifying how to do the work so we don't reinvent the wheel. Standard processes promote efficiency. Once you have a process, you optimize it to lower costs and raise profit margins.

Business and HR leaders focus a lot of time and energy on maintaining processes so that customers efficiently get their products and services every day ("keeping the lights on"). Financial controls ensure that budgets are not overrun, and process controls ensure efficiency of operations. Human capital policies and procedures ensure that talent is available when and where the business needs it and that employees are motivated to do the work.

Unfortunately, simplification and standard processes are not enough. You have to recognize and manage the organizational complexity for successful strategy execution. There are always multiple strategic and operational objectives that are in conflict with each other. Increase market share, but don't spend too much money doing it. Innovate, but make sure the prices are affordable for the customer. Provide high quality customer service, but don't spend too much time on each customer. Minimize warehouse inventory, but don't create shortages for the customers. Attract new customers, but don't cut prices too much. And so on.

The challenge for frontline and middle managers is how to deal with the competing strategic and operational objectives. If you follow one process too zealously, you take time and energy away from other operational and strategic goals.

Consider the following exchange between Michelle, Operations VP, and Trent, her HR business partner.

> Trent: *"Michelle, your team really needs to follow the performance management process. We're seeing lots of gaps in compliance, and the HR leadership team is giving me a hard time. And next week don't forget about our quarterly review of your direct reports' career plans and the succession plans for key roles."*
>
> Michelle: *"I keep telling them to get the reviews done. But we're just so crazy busy with all the business priorities. Unless the company makes more money, all this HR stuff is going to be irrelevant. We'll have to start cutting headcount."*

Exchanges like this occur every day worldwide in companies in all industries. The specific business and HR priorities vary, but the essence of the problem is the same: they are not aligned. Business leaders focus on strategy execution and don't pay enough attention to organizational effectiveness, while HR leaders do the opposite. The consequence: bottom line results suffer.

The key to strategic success is striking the right balance between competing priorities. Doing Strategic Analytics helps you determine that balance.

The problem with doing only business analytics or only HR analytics. A thousand things can be improved in existing programs and processes, but only a handful are truly strategic. Using business analytics to focus on refining existing processes misses the larger picture of weaknesses created by the work design, the annual operating plan, and the budgeting process. Human capital analytics that focus on improving HR programs face huge challenges of knowing where to start.

Table 1 summarizes the strengths and weaknesses of the enterprise and human capital approaches to analytics and decision making. People like Michelle, who use only the enterprise analytics approach, often mistakenly assume that people will behave a particular way just because they are told to. However, people are not robots to be programmed or widgets that can be effortlessly moved from one task to another. The complementary human capital approach is needed to shed light on what drives behavior for individuals. The solutions are almost always more nuanced and complex than senior leaders want to believe.

	Business / Enterprise approach	HR / Human capital approach
Focus	Strategy execution	Organizational effectiveness
Strength	Operational metrics that are closely aligned with strategy execution	Talent management
Weakness	Ensuring the right roles, skills, and behaviors are developed and deployed at the individual level	Ensuring the individual level behaviors and roles are tightly aligned with group performance that contributes directly to strategy execution
Blind spot	Strategists and senior leaders assume frontline managers and employees will exhibit the right behaviors just because they tell them to.	Saving money by being more efficient can cripple strategic capability. Don't cut for the sake of cutting just because you can positively impact cash flow in the short term.

Table 1: The Enterprise and Human Capital Approaches Compared

People like Trent, who use only human capital analytics, frequently have the mistaken belief that showing a financial impact is the same as improving strategic capability. Saving money by being more efficient with current HR processes says nothing about whether they are the right ones for strategic success. The complementary enterprise approach is needed to ensure alignment with strategic objectives.

Strategic impact or ROI? The fact that HR is challenged to justify the return on investment (ROI) of its programs is just one part of a larger problem with the way ROI is used in organizations. ROI focuses on cash flow. The only benefits that can be included in ROI have to be expressed in monetary terms.

The organizational capabilities that create competitive advantage ultimately increase cash flow. But their effect is not always direct or immediate. Building the capability to deliver on strategic goals, such as better customer service, quality, innovation, and others, can have very strong impacts on business success, which is why they are part of the strategy. However, the immediate effect on ROI is usually negative: you spend money to invest in the capabilities, with no guarantee of financial payback.

For example, Facebook for years focused on building an enormous user base even though it hadn't figured out how to monetize that base. Their strategy was very clear: they knew exactly what organization capabilities they needed to execute the strategy, and they invested very heavily in those capabilities. Ultimately there was a huge financial payoff after they deployed advertising. However, when Facebook initially built their user base support capabilities, there was no way to either calculate or forecast ROI in a meaningful way.

Facebook is an extreme example that nonetheless proves the point. Building organization capability to execute the strategy is not equivalent to showing increased financial ROI in the short term; they can be in opposition to each other, at least in the initial stages of capability building. Strategic Analytics focuses on what it takes to build that capability, not ROI.

Get your strategic priorities straight. Strategic priorities can have conflicting impacts on profitability: there is tension between the strategic priority and the need to keep costs down to make money. For many consumer products companies, the priority is low finished product cost and high quality. For technology and pharmaceutical companies, it's cutting-edge innovation that doesn't cost too much to create. For many consumer and financial services firms, it's cost-effective customer service. Safety is a primary concern in manufacturing, mining, and construction—but you can overspend on safety to the point where you see few to no additional safety gains while margins erode. And so on.

The tension often gets translated into "do more with less." Problems in strategy execution arise when the benchmarks that senior leaders use to set productivity and quality targets cannot be attained within the allocated budgets. In most organizations, that's close to a daily occurrence. Figuring out why productivity or quality is falling short, or why costs are exceeding budgets, takes up inordinate amounts of time for middle and frontline managers. They rarely arrive at the best diagnoses and solutions because they don't know how to incorporate what's going on with the people.

The answer is an integrated approach that looks at the entire system—the business and HR processes, the strategic and human capital objectives, the way work is organized and carried out, all of it—to determine the root causes of the problems. For example, boosting productivity and quality typically happens one of two ways: through substituting technology for people or redesigning the work (or both). Work redesign that boosts productivity and quality usually is most successful when done using high-performance work design principles (chapters 5, 6, and 10). Successfully designing, implementing and managing a system like that requires looking at business and people processes together.

Strategic Analytics one step at a time. Before you decide I'm asking you to do the analytics equivalent of climbing Mount

Everest, please know the following: you don't have to climb the highest mountain to get better insights into virtually *all* the strategic and performance issues facing your organization. The Strategic Analytics framework provides a practical, step-by-step guide to deeper and more actionable insights than the analytics currently practiced in most corners of your organization. Just by defining the problem and identifying the most likely causes—building the causal model—you will be in a position to make better decisions, even if you don't have enough time and resources for high-powered statistical analysis. In fact, in most cases there often is no justification for rocket scientist level statistics. Qualitative analysis alone, using stakeholder interviews, often is the only thing you need to get actionable insights.

This book shows how to use Strategic Analytics to get better alignment between the business and HR. You will find specific details on the different parts of both enterprise and human capital analytics that have to be conducted for successful integration. Guidance on the specific questions to ask is included, along with examples of how to do the analytics. Strategic Analytics is a team sport. You can't get to the deepest insights without both the business and HR perspectives on the team doing the analysis together.

It's all about the system. Strategic Analytics is a type of systems analysis: you look at the entire system to determine what's driving behavior. When you understand the link to the larger system, you can properly diagnose the root causes of behavior and motivation. It's also the surest way to find changes to solve the problems instead of temporary solutions that only paper over the root causes.

A key to Strategic Analytics is doing the analytics in the right order. Both business and HR leaders tell the story of how organizational performance occurs by starting with people's contributions (human capital performance). Their contributions combine with others to create business processes (enterprise performance), and this combination in turn leads to strategy execution. If strategy isn't executed properly, we look for the things specific people and roles could do differently. This chain of events is shown in figure 1: the causation runs from human capital to enterprise performance and ultimately to strategy execution.

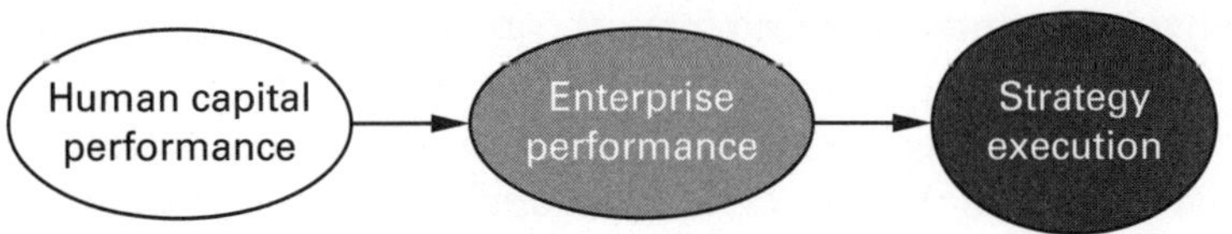

Figure 1: Telling the Story of How Strategy Execution Occurs

The challenge is figuring out what to focus on. There are so many things that can be improved at the job level, including screening, training, promotions, performance management, coaching, integrating jobs with each other, goal setting, and so on. It's easy to tell a story where improving on any of those

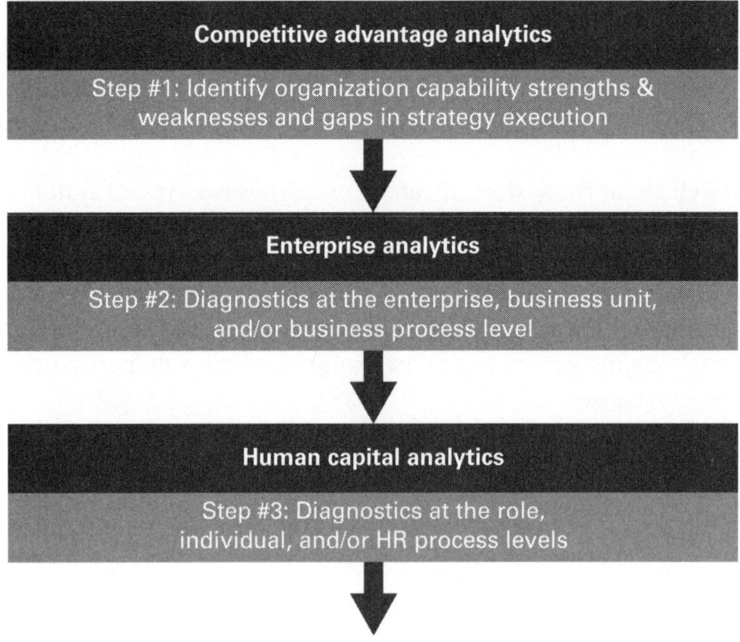

Figure 2: Strategic Analytics Roadmap

dimensions *could* help improve human capital performance and thus enterprise performance and strategy execution. The challenge is identifying which ones matter most. For that, you have to order the analysis the other way around.

A complete Strategic Analytics diagnostic follows the sequence outlined in figure 2. There are three steps:

- Step 1—Competitive Advantage Analytics: The process starts with the strategy. What creates your competitive advantage—how do you make money and preserve your position in the marketplace? In the first step you (a) identify the organizational strengths and weaknesses that define competitive advantage, (b) build a causal model that lays out the details, and (c) get alignment with key stakeholders on the need for analysis. A key part of this step is figuring out where people get too wrapped up in focusing on specific business processes and lose sight of the strategic objectives.
- Step 2—Enterprise Analytics: For the second step you test the causal model at the appropriate level of enterprise analysis: at the organization-wide level, at the business unit level, or at the business process level. At this step the analytics use metrics and stakeholder interviews to understand where the organization is falling short on meeting its strategic objectives. High-powered statistics are rarely, if ever, needed here.
- Step 3—Human Capital Analytics: The third step augments the enterprise analysis with human capital analysis as needed, doing diagnostics at the role, individual, or HR process levels. The analytics at this step can include advanced statistics if the data are available and that type of analysis is relevant. More than half the battle in getting to actionable insights is defining the right questions and making sure you don't focus on the wrong data, not applying advanced statistics.

Step 1 is the most straightforward and most important—and it's precisely what people fail to do all the time. If you jump straight into either enterprise or human capital analysis, you can easily miss the critical link that ties business and people issues together. You need step 1 to tell the difference between insights that offer only marginal improvements in operations and the ones that truly advance strategy.

For those of you who like to think mostly in terms of what goes on with individual workers, Strategic Analytics boils down to the following. Do the people who are responsible for delivering the organization's products and services have the responsibility, skills, motivation, coordination, and support to keep the system going and simultaneously advance the strategy? If the answer is yes, then the system is designed properly. If no, then Strategic Analytics identifies what needs to change.

Do as much as you can, and you still will benefit. The Strategic Analytics approach does not have to be onerous, just comprehensive. Depending on the issue you're investigating and the time and resources available, you can easily adapt the framework and achieve deeper insights than you'd get otherwise. The benefit of the approach is better informed decision making, even if you don't have permission to make changes to address structural issues.

The first main benefit of Strategic Analytics is avoiding solutions that won't work due to factors beyond your control. For example, suppose the strategy execution problem is low productivity in a role. You are asked to improve the employees' morale and engagement under the assumption that productivity will also improve. Suppose further that you are told to focus on solutions that don't involve increasing pay. Faced with those restrictions, most people in organizations would exclude compensation from the analysis. After all, if you can't increase pay, why focus on it as a potential cause? The answer is that pay may matter a lot. If it does, then leaving it unchanged could keep you from achieving the productivity goals.

Strategic Analytics casts a broad net, taking into account all potential factors, which in this case includes compensation. Suppose the diagnostic reveals that low compensation creates problems in attracting and retaining high-quality talent. There may be some small changes you could make to marginally improve employee morale and engagement. But without a compensation increase, a large competency gap will exist, because you're not paying enough to attract and retain the right people. Doing Strategic Analytics gives you the information you need to tell senior leaders that focusing on morale and engagement alone almost certainly won't achieve the desired productivity improvement.

For another example, consider the case study from chapter 7 on evaluating the business impact of executive coaching. Most executive coaching engagements tend to focus on leadership behaviors that may help the leader to communicate and manage the team better, but they offer no guarantee of improved strategy execution. Doing the Strategic Analytics diagnostic on executive coaching can reveal which leadership competencies are more likely to improve execution.

The second benefit comes from setting the organization up for deeper analytics and insights later on. Given the short amount of time allowed ("get it done yesterday"), there are limits on how long you can take to do the analysis. Building the causal model and doing some initial analysis may be all that you can finish within the time constraints. After meeting the immediate deadline for recommendations, you can do a deeper analysis into the complete set of factors you identified as potential contributors. I have used this approach many times in my work with companies. I provide preliminary conclusions based on a partial analysis to satisfy an immediate demand for decision making. I then conduct the more in-depth analysis over a longer period and have the results ready when new urgent deadlines related to the organizational issues crop up.

One note about terminology: I use both "business analytics" and "enterprise analytics" to refer to the same thing: analysis focused on the organization, business unit, or work group (region, site, team, etc.) levels. "HR analytics" and "human capital analytics" also are used interchangeably to refer to analytics at the role or individual levels.

The limits of Strategic Analytics. A Strategic Analytics diagnostic addresses strategy execution challenges that arise from internal factors. The factors that are covered include the organization design, culture, allocation of decision rights, matrix structures, cross-functional collaboration, (high-performance) job design, individual competencies, motivation, and more. Because these are internal factors, in principle they can be changed and controlled. I do not claim that changing any of these factors is easy, only that it is feasible.

What Strategic Analytics does not address is the role of external factors in strategy failure, nor problems with the strategy itself. Many strategies fail not because of flaws in the organization but because the strategy itself is ill conceived. Any strategy that requires deviating from the organization's established capabilities and market strengths carries a risk of failure because of competitive pressures beyond the leadership's control. For example, a company that tries to enter an entirely new line of business that is very different from its core competency faces a very small chance of success. No amount of reorganization, culture change, overhaul of existing staff, or tweaking of processes will radically increase the chances of success. The best organization design can't save a bad strategy.

Target audience. There are three main audiences for this book: leaders, frontline managers, and analysts.

For senior business and HR leaders, Strategic Analytics can help you better orient how your organization approaches diagnosing and solving problems with strategy execution. It can improve the approach you take, as well as the analytics others conduct under your guidance. Use the framework to push for cross-functional analysis and solutions to challenges in performance and strategy execution.

For frontline business and HR managers, Strategic Analytics can help broaden how you think about the organizational system and the behavioral drivers of strategic success. You are not likely to lead an in-depth analysis yourself, but you can challenge others to do more than just enterprise or human capital analytics. Use the framework to push back, where appropriate, when you are given predetermined solutions that are based on incomplete diagnostics.

For business and HR analysts, Strategic Analytics can be a template for doing much more comprehensive and insightful work. You are not always given permission to cast a broad net when designing your diagnostic. Strategic Analytics shows the importance of doing so for understanding *all* the true drivers of successful business performance and strategy execution. Use the framework to deliver actionable insights that challenge senior leadership to think, act, and budget differently than the status quo.

Organization of the book. The book is organized as follows. Part I addresses why Strategic Analytics is the right approach. Chapter 1 covers the importance of building and testing causal models and the dangers of incomplete data analysis. A robust causal model for diagnosing strategy execution problems is presented, tying together factors that impact business performance at both the individual and group levels.

A properly specified causal model identifies the leading factors that *should* improve strategy execution. When doing the analytics, those factors are recast as hypotheses: questions about strategy execution that need to be formally tested. The causal model narrows down the list of candidate factors (hypotheses) to the ones that are most likely to drive the desired results.

Chapter 2 addresses problems with using ROI to evaluate business and HR decisions. A critical issue is the tradeoff between short-term increases in cash flow versus longer-term impacts on competitive advantage. Competitive advantage ultimately leads to increased cash flow in the long run, but at the cost of short-term cash flow as investments are made. Additional common metrics besides ROI are reviewed and critiqued.

Part II details the steps of how to do Strategic Analytics.

Chapter 3 explains the order for conducting the analytics, plus a range of topics you should know before getting started, including (a) how Strategic Analytics is related to balanced scorecards, (b) the importance of interviews and qualitative analysis, and (c) who should construct the causal model. Qualitative enterprise analysis is often all that is needed to deliver actionable insights. And even if no in-depth analysis is conducted, laying out the causal model is very important. If you don't have a lot of time, a properly constructed causal model still can help improve decision making.

Chapter 4 covers step 1 in the Strategic Analytics process: identifying the sources of competitive advantage, including the organization capability strengths and weaknesses, and focusing the enterprise and human capital analysis on those. A thousand things can be done that might help improve organizational performance and strategy execution. Focusing your attention on organizational capabilities that provide competitive advantage is most critical for successful strategy execution; doing so narrows the inquiry to a manageable set of truly causal factors to be analyzed.

Chapter 5 covers step 2 in the Strategic Analytics process: enterprise analytics, which diagnose performance barriers and enablers at the enterprise, business unit, and/or business process levels. These analytics focus on alignment and gaps in the organization design, organization capabilities, and culture. Specific questions to be addressed for each of the three components of enterprise analytics are provided.

Chapter 6 covers step 3 in the Strategic Analytics process: human capital analytics, which diagnose performance barriers and enablers at the role, individual, and/or HR process levels. These analytics focus on alignment and gaps in the areas of job design, individual competencies, and motivation and attitudes. Specific questions to be addressed for each of the three components of human capital analytics are provided.

Chapter 7 presents Strategic Analytics case studies. It provides examples of three different types of diagnostic: (a) cases where only enterprise analysis needs to be conducted rigorously (minimal human capital analysis), (b) cases where human capital analysis is the primary focus (minimal enterprise analysis), and (c) cases where both types of analysis take time and effort.

The examples show how the type of diagnostic depends on the context and questions being addressed. It should not depend on the personal preferences and biases of the people leading the analysis: business leaders should not focus only on enterprise analysis because that's what they are familiar with, or vice versa for HR professionals and human capital analysis.

Chapter 8 covers a specific application of the framework: customer retention and profitable growth. It provides a detailed example of how to apply integrated enterprise and human capital analytics for large commercial banks, technology companies, and retail sales companies.

Chapter 9 covers another specific application: go-to-market (GTM) strategies and effectiveness. Specific case studies from the package delivery and logistics industry and from consumer product direct-store-delivery (DSD) systems are discussed in detail.

Part III dives more deeply into specific topical areas of current practice. It reviews where common practice is already consistent with Strategic Analytics and where it can be improved.

Chapter 10 addresses critical roles, group performance, and competencies. How do we identify top talent and high potentials? What is the contribution of the employee versus the group versus the leader in driving behaviors and performance? How do organizations balance higher pay for high performance with the need to economize on compensation costs?

Chapter 11 covers making sense of sensing data. Many of the early warning signs of organizational issues arise from employee surveys and other data that raise questions about culture and organizational effectiveness. Specific examples are illustrated using case studies on speed of decision making and on innovativeness.

Chapter 12 addresses human capital development and retention analytics. How do you know if the capabilities being built will enable strategy execution? The chapter includes a critique of the two dominant approaches to evaluating human capital development activities: ROI analysis and the Kirkpatrick model. An alternative approach based on a causal model of performance is provided.

The last chapter concludes with a summary of key learning and action points from the book.

The appendix provides a diagnostic interview template for conducting Strategic Analytics. You can use it to design a diagnostic that is relevant for whatever issue you want to address. The questions and details for the diagnostic are drawn from the core chapters of the book.

STRATEGIC ANALYTICS

Part I

Why Do Strategic Analytics?

This first part of the book lays out the case for why you should do analytics that integrate the enterprise (business) and human capital (people) perspectives.

Chapter 1 addresses the importance of building and testing causal models and the dangers of incomplete analysis. Chapter 2 addresses problems with ROI and other common metrics as tools for evaluating both business and HR decisions.

A main argument for doing Strategic Analytics is that you will build your diagnostic in the right order. Leaders like to tell the story of how organizational performance is achieved by starting with the people who make it happen. That's fine for storytelling and drawing people into the narrative. But if you start the analysis at the human capital level, you can quickly get lost in the myriad problems that are rampant in most roles and business processes. There are a thousand things you can fix, but only a handful of these are truly strategic. Strategic Analytics starts with the strategy you are trying to achieve and the organizational capability needed to support the strategy. You first analyze those, and then you turn to human capital analytics if needed.

Chapter 1

Of Elephants and Incomplete Analytics

Issues Addressed in This Chapter

- Most analytics conducted today by the business and by HR are incomplete and cannot solve strategy execution problems on their own
- You need a full causal model to diagnose the entire system and to understand what really drives behavior and performance

Key Questions

- What problems are you trying to solve with your analysis?
- How does the analysis you have chosen help to improve strategy execution?

You need to know what drives performance in your organization to get strategy execution right. The problem with organizational analytics today is that they tell an incomplete story. Enterprise analytics and human capital analytics are conducted along parallel and separate tracks. Both attempt to determine why performance happens, yet each on its own can tell only part of the story. Without the complete story, we don't really know the best ways to improve strategy execution and organizational effectiveness.

Enterprise analytics can tell us if we're achieving the strategy and details about the operational measures that contribute to strategy execution. A typical analysis addresses questions like these:

- What types of customers can best help increase our share in existing markets?
- What new markets can we succeed in?
- What organizational capabilities do we need for strategic success?

The enterprise metrics used to answer these questions include market share, sales, and margins, among others, and extend to operational and technical measures that describe business processes, such as productivity, innovation, quality, manufacturing uptime, time-to-market, customer service, and others.

On the human capital side, a typical analysis tries to figure out the sources of organizational ineffectiveness, focusing almost exclusively on how work is done and whether people work well together. A typical analysis addresses questions like these:

- Who are our best leaders, and what role do they really play?
- Is a group or team performing well or working at cross purposes?
- What is the right mix of compensation versus nonmonetary rewards in motivating performance?
- How can we improve our HR practices to be more effective?

The human capital metrics used to answer these questions include leadership and frontline worker competencies, employee attitudes, and measures of human resource (HR) program efficiency and effectiveness.

Enterprise analytics tells us whether the strategy is executed. But it can't tell us which jobs and individual-level behaviors most directly lead to improved strategy execution. The human capital perspective is essential, but only on rare occasions are people from the human capital side invited to contribute when senior leaders conduct business analytics. Instead, they usually are told what happened only after the key decisions were made.

Business analytics and HR analytics as commonly practiced are examples of incomplete analysis: they do not specify and test a full causal model. Rather than looking at the entire system that defines and drives organizational performance, they take shortcuts and focus on too few elements. To illustrate the problem with the analysis of large complex systems based on only partial data, consider the scene in figure 3, which is from a centuries-old fable.

Figure 3: The Perils of Incomplete Data Analysis

The scene is a group of blind monks who are each touching different parts of an elephant. Modern versions of the story star blind men, and sometimes only three of them, though the specific stars of the story are not important. What matters is the analysis performed by each person, which occurs in isolation and without consideration of the data gathered by the other people.

WHAT'S THE RIGHT LEVEL OF CUSTOMER SERVICE? A SYSTEMS DIAGNOSIS APPROACH.

Business-to-consumer industries. Determining the right amount of customer service is a challenge for all organizations. If you don't provide enough, key customers walk out the door. If you provide too much, profit margins get whittled down to nothing and you don't make any money.

Customer service in business-to-consumer industries is driven by product quality, ease of use, and responsiveness of customer service representatives (CSRs). When customer service scores fall, the directive to operational leaders may simply be "Go figure out how to get customer service back to where it was before." Suppose product development previously decided to save costs by reducing spending on quality assurance processes. They may have assessed that existing processes are redundant, slowing time to market and reducing sales. If the lower spending on quality assurance is misguided, the end result would be lower product quality and unhappy customers. If the customer service scores do not measure product quality, fingers could be pointed at the CSRs, leading to the incorrect conclusion that they had become less motivated to provide high-quality customer service.

For another case, consider the link between CSR compensation and customer service. Suppose the customer service site leader is held accountable for metrics such as time to resolve customer complaints and efficiency of the operations (call volume, wait times, and similar issues). If she does not have profit and loss (P&L) responsibility for her operations she will push for higher compensation for her CSRs as a way to attract and retain higher skilled employees. Similarly, HR might advocate for greater pay to reduce attrition and improve retention of the longer-tenured and more experienced CSRs. However, evaluating whether better pay is worth the investment requires a complete Strategic Analytics diagnostic that addresses the relationship between customer retention and sales and profitability.

Business-to-business industries. In business-to-business industries, customer service involves striking the right balance between cutting prices to make the sale and maximizing profits. A Strategic Analytics diagnostic looks at the complete set of interactions between the customer and organization, along with the role played by each employee and function. For example, salespeople may be given discretion to set specific contract terms, but they need timely and accurate information on how the terms impact enterprise profitability through metrics such as capacity utilization. And they need to be trained and evaluated on overall profitability, not just sales.

The person touching the tail concludes that an elephant has features like a rope. The person touching the leg thinks the elephant's shape is more like a tree. The person touching the tusk has no idea what the elephant's skin feels like. And so on. All their conclusions seem reasonable, given the information at each person's disposal, but all fail to describe the entire animal properly.

Enterprise analytics today are like the person touching only the head. They are out in front, focusing on a part of the animal that is pointed forward. Yet trying to dictate the direction and pace of the animal by focusing only the head can be a lost cause. If the animal's legs are tethered to a post, it cannot move, no matter what you do. You may point the animal in the right direction, but you will never get it to move forward.

Human capital analytics today are like the person touching only the hind legs. They move in unison with other parts of the body, but they contribute only one part to the animal's full range of motion and have no effect on direction. You can't properly diagnose problems with overall direction and speed by ignoring the rest of the animal and analyzing just the rear legs.

What's missing from both types of analysis is the rest of the body: the front legs that work in unison with the rear legs to propel the body forward and the torso that holds it all together. Excluding the trunk leaves out key information about how the animal maintains its health through eating, drinking, and bathing. Enterprise and human capital analytics, when conducted separately, fall short of identifying and testing a complete causal model. The most accurate insights require a combined analysis that diagnoses the performance drivers for the entire system, not just one part of it.

Data mining is not causal analysis. One of the biggest mistakes I see frequently is simple data analysis that focuses on only one or two pieces of information. The problem is that simple analysis without a causal model can lead to the wrong conclusions: it is just data mining and not science. A typical example is when consultants look at a group of companies and conclude that "the use of HR practice XYZ is more common at high-performing companies," where XYZ could be the latest leadership development program, incentive pay philosophy, employee engagement strategy, and so on. The implication is that if your organization adopts the same practice, your business results will improve. The implicit causal model is shown in figure 4.

The problem is that HR practices by themselves do not create business results. They are one contribution in a larger system that enables the business results. HR practices can improve

Figure 4: An Overly Simple Causal Model of HR Practices and Strategy Execution

strategy execution only when they are aligned with other parts of the system.

Consider the following incomplete analysis example. To start, let's say that customer retention drops, triggering alarm bells. A quick scan of available data might reveal that at approximately the same time there was an increase in turnover among customer service agents. Putting those two pieces of information side by side, many people would conclude that the increase in agent turnover "caused" the drop in customer retention. But consider some alternative explanations and data:

- What if the increase in turnover was concentrated among low-performing agents? In this case the turnover might have been caused by the drop in customer retention, not the other way around, as managers attempted to address low retention through improved customer service.
- What if there was a recent change in the managerial team at a big call center where many agents work? A new leadership team might be inexperienced and unable to maintain previous levels of both customer satisfaction and employee engagement, leading both to fall simultaneously.
- What if a new customer relationship management (CRM) system was recently introduced? Problems with getting a new system to work properly could drive both customers and employees to leave.
- What if the external labor market for agents has been heating up in recent months? Failure to keep up with the market in terms of pay, benefits, and developmental opportunities can drive turnover.
- What if there has been a steady decline in employee engagement scores on the annual survey? Longer-term trends in employee wellbeing could either be unrelated to the recent loss of customers—or a direct contributor to it.

Each of these alternatives is a hypothesis about the relationship between customer retention and employee turnover. Each hypothesis was formed by introducing additional pieces of information to the original empirical observation that customer retention and employee turnover are statistically related. The problem is that each piece of data on its own is not enough to test these hypotheses. A Strategic Analytics causal model is needed to combine all relevant information together for joint testing.

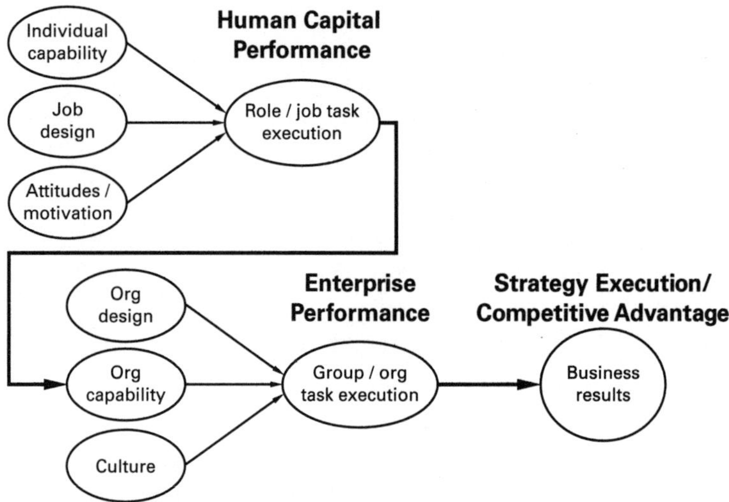

Figure 5: A Causal Model of Human Capital and Enterprise Performance

Figure 5 presents a causal model you can use for the Strategic Analytics diagnostic. The model is used throughout the book to show how to conduct integrated analytics. It features two main parts: human capital (or individual) performance in the top half and enterprise (or organizational) performance in the bottom half, with the arrows indicating casual pathways. Individual capability, job design (roles and responsibilities), and attitudes (motivation) combine to produce human capital performance. Enterprise performance occurs when people in their individual roles do their jobs according to the organization design, creating the organizational capability through their actions, with culture acting as a catalyst.

For most strategic objectives in almost all industries, successful execution requires the combined efforts of multiple people in different roles working together as a team. That means considering both the top and bottom parts of the causal model in figure 5.

For some roles in organizations, the top part of the causal model in figure 5 is all that is needed. These roles directly contribute to strategy execution with minimal reliance on or interdependence with other roles. For example, if individual salespeople can (almost) singlehandedly increase sales, then the top part of the causal model may be sufficient to analyze sales performance. If the objective of your strategy is customer satisfaction and retention, then the top part of the causal model may also be sufficient for customer service agents. Other examples that focus primarily on human capital performance with little to no emphasis on enterprise performance are covered in chapter 7's case studies on retaining critical talent (figure 12) and evaluating the impact of executive coaching (figure 13).

Group, team, site, business unit, or organizational performance all can be addressed with the bottom part of the causal model in figure 5. The contribution of all roles together within the context of culture creates the task execution for the group, which in turn leads to the business results (strategy execution). In some cases, you can focus the analytics exclusively at the enterprise level and pay little to no attention to the human capital level. Examples from chapter 7 include the case studies on speed of decision making (figure 11) and role redundancy.

Examples where both in-depth enterprise and human capital analysis are needed include chapter 7's case studies on route sales maximization (figure 14) and business unit optimization (figure 15). These require more time and are harder to conduct than the other two types—analysis primarily only at the human capital or only at the enterprise levels. Which type of analysis you choose to conduct, though, needs to be driven by the information you need for a proper systems diagnosis, not by expediency.

Figure 5 is simultaneously simple yet powerful. It is simple enough that it can be used to describe how business performance can be achieved for virtually any strategic objective or organizational process. It is powerful because the multiple levels of analysis can yield the critical insights needed to boost performance and improve execution of your strategy. For example, consider the hypotheses about the link between customer retention and customer service agent turnover from earlier in this chapter:

- Increased turnover of low-performing agents means an increase in average agent capability, a factor in the upper left part of the model.
- A recent change in the managerial team at a big call center means a change in the organizational support the agents at that call center receive, which could show up as a change in attitudes and behaviors at the individual level and/or culture and behaviors at the group (call center) levels.
- Problems implementing a new customer relationship management (CRM) system, a change in the job design, could show up as either an increased or decreased ability to perform the job tasks.
- More outside employment opportunities would make it harder to attract and retain high-quality agents.
- A steady decline in employee engagement scores means worse attitudes.

Each individual piece of data that was used to try and determine a link between customer service agent turnover and customer retention represents one or more elements of the causal model in figure 5. Focusing on only one piece of data at a time just because it "makes sense" or "feels right" is no substitute for building the complete causal model. Though the hypotheses derived from individual pieces of data may all be reasonable in isolation, you need integrated analysis to determine the true causes of strategy execution.

In certain situations, like some of the case studies presented in chapter 7, you won't end up doing extensive analysis at one of the two levels—either at the enterprise level or at the human capital level. However, you need the first step in Strategic Analytics to reliably determine if you can focus primarily on only one of those two levels. If competitive advantage analytics show that it's sufficient to do extensive analysis only at one of the two levels, that's fine. In contrast, skipping over step 1 and focusing on only enterprise or human capital analytics just because you are pressed for time or because you're not familiar with the other approach is not.

Part II addresses how to do the analysis. But before we get to that, chapter 2 takes a look at ROI and other common analysis tools. Their deficiencies highlight the value of doing Strategic Analytics.

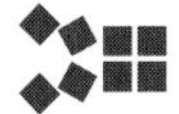

Chapter 2

Beware the ROI Bogeyman and Other Monsters under the Bed

Issues Addressed in This Chapter

- ROI is not effective as a decision-making tool to improve strategy execution and organizational effectiveness.
- You can improve short-term cash flow (and ROI) if you stop investing in the organizational capability that provides your competitive advantage in the long run.
- Other common measurements are no better than ROI, confusing correlation with causation.

Key Questions

- Are we trying to improve short-term cash flow or long-term competitive advantage?
- Which strategic benefits cannot be easily linked to increased cash flow today?

Return on investment (ROI) is perhaps the most universally applied tool ever created in the history of finance. It is a standard measurement used to evaluate the financial return from an investment or project.

For all its power, though, ROI is a lot like the monster or bogeyman hiding under the bed that young children fear. It can seem big and scary, even at times all powerful, when we are young. But when we grow up and can see things with a broader perspective, we understand the reality and can put our youthful fears to rest. ROI today is used like a litmus test for HR—if HR cannot show a high enough ROI, then Finance will never approve what HR wants to do. And HR is like the young child fearing the ROI bogeyman under the bed: it doesn't have the right perspective on the limitations of ROI and what should be done instead. The analytics I propose here provide an answer.

To show why ROI doesn't live up to the promise it's supposed to have for evaluating HR, I first have to address why it's lacking as a tool for making business decisions.

The problem with ROI as a business decision tool. For the sake of this discussion, let's divide the world of investment decisions into two parts: investing in something the organization has done successfully in the past versus investing in something the organization has never tried before (even if other companies have done so). For things you've done successfully in the past, ROI is a fine way to assign a value to the expected financial return. Your past experience with these types of investment ensures high levels of certainty and low risk regarding their success and the costs needed to get there. Examples include opening up a new office, factory, or retail outlet under conditions that are similar to what your company has experienced in the past, or rolling out new equipment and machinery at sites using technology already tried and tested at pilot sites.

ROI also can be appropriate for evaluating activities that help maintain operations. This can apply to both capital expenditures and HR. If HR determines that the company needs to invest in employee compensation, training, or something else in order to maintain its current capability and operational performance, the ROI in terms of avoiding a hit to existing operations can often be demonstrated. For example, suppose that turnover among high-performing sales people increases because the market for their skills ramps up and competitors start poaching them. To keep them, the company may have to raise compensation, perhaps significantly more than the annual plan has room for. The financial return from increasing their compensation is expressed as the loss in sales that is avoided.

Avoiding lost sales is a clear financial benefit that can be included in ROI in this case. However, not all degradations in employee capability can be directly traced to lost sales. Consider another case, where the customer market shifts and accounts become more complex (more complex contract terms, greater geographic coverage, tighter timelines, or some other situation), requiring greater cross-functional collaboration between sales, marketing, customer service, and IT. It may be next to impossible to establish a direct link between the need for better collaboration and an immediate impact on sales or customer retention. Nonetheless, the collaboration is essential to maintain competitive advantage.

This example and the exhibit ("Calculating the ROI of New Product Development") help demonstrate why ROI is not the preferred measure when the organization is doing something new. When an investment or changes in organizational capability have an uncertain and/or indirect, future-oriented impact on customer satisfaction and potential sales, something different than ROI is needed.

CALCULATING THE ROI OF NEW PRODUCT DEVELOPMENT

Calculating the ROI of new product development is like reading tea leaves—and just as accurate.

New product development is highly risky and uncertain. You never really know what's going to happen until after you've been through the development process. The total resources and time needed are forecast at the front end before you start, but inevitably fall short. The budget overruns and missed deadlines happen simply because you don't know what you don't know.

You can calculate the expected ROI of new product development, but all the assumptions that go into the calculation are just that—assumptions. The assumptions are made using imperfect data amid enormous uncertainty about what the market for the product ultimately will look like and what resources really will be needed to get there. The uncertainty and assumptions make ROI unreliable as a decision aid. Despite that, senior leaders don't shy away from making big bets on new product development. They do it because they have to; otherwise competitors can attack your margins and market share. They just don't use ROI as a finely honed decision making tool—it is one of a number of things that factor into decision making about new product development (along with anticipated market size, pricing/margins, ability to win sales over competitors, and so on).

A more comprehensive analysis than traditional ROI requires building a detailed causal model. The model must include the key organizational processes that have to work properly for the investment to succeed, including the role that people's capabilities, motivation, and job design will play in the investment's success. The analysis would then assess the strength of the relationship between the causal factors and strategic and financial outcomes. It also should differentiate between financial benefits achieved through shorter-term cash flow improvements versus longer term capability building.

Increasing and maintaining competitive advantage are the ultimate objectives of strategy. If you have competitive advantage, revenue and cash flow are a direct result. But the causation does not go the other way around: increases in revenue and cash flow do not necessarily mean an increase in competitive advantage. Why? Because you can increase cash flow by cutting short-term investments in the very strategic capability you are trying to build over the longer term (figure 6).

Consider spending on a new IT system that is due to launch in three years. If you want to boost short-term cash flow, you can defer some spending on the new IT system. And if you assume the short-term spending cuts won't impact the ultimate project delivery (because you found ways to do the work more efficiently), then you can show a positive ROI from the spending cuts: the forecast for revenue stays the same while costs are lower, so profit has increased. Yet what proof do you have that making those budget cuts will not have a negative impact on the functionality and usefulness of the new IT system and thus on potential future revenue? Unless the proof is ironclad, you can't assume that.

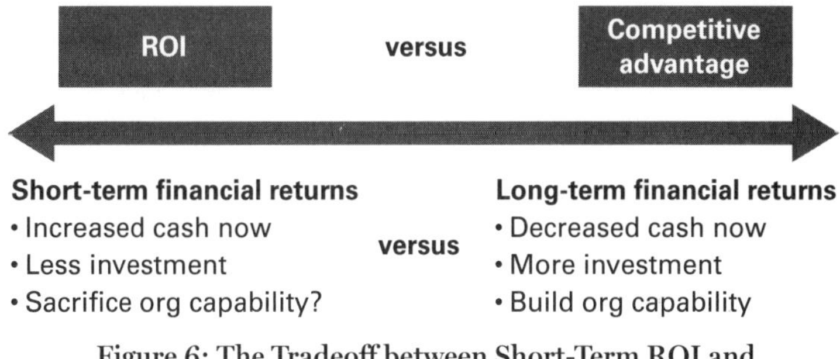

Figure 6: The Tradeoff between Short-Term ROI and Long-Term Competitive Advantage

This tradeoff between the certainties of increased short-term cash flow from spending reductions versus the uncertain impact on longer-term strategic capability is precisely why ROI alone is never sufficient to guide strategic investment decisions. The easiest way to increase short-term cash flow (and thus ROI) is to cut spending on investment to improve capability, the organizational equivalent of cutting off your nose to spite your face—it can be done but it's not very advisable. It's also why ROI should never be the only measure used to assess spending on human capital or HR programs, if those programs are supposed to improve organizational capability.

The problem with ROI as a tool for evaluating human capital. HR is often asked to show the ROI of its programs and processes. Think about how this usually plays out. When applied to human capital or HR, ROI is almost always used defensively to justify programs and policies for which there is not enthusiastic support. At the same time, there often is unwavering support for people and processes that key stakeholders "know" are critical for strategic success. So if ROI is not the preferred method for understanding how people and processes contribute to strategic success, what is? And how can organizations better diagnose what levers they need to pull to improve strategy execution and organizational effectiveness?

For example, effective strategy execution often can be improved through better communication about goals and priorities. An HR objective of better communication about goals and priorities can lessen the amount of time needed to complete work processes, which in turn can improve resource use efficiency—a monetary benefit that can be included in ROI. However, the benefits of better communication do not necessarily show up directly and immediately in more efficient use of resources. Instead, more efficient use of resources is often realized only after a significant delay following the improved communication, or in conjunction with other interventions such as team coaching, improved leadership and IT support, or changes in the work design. The benefit of improved communication can be expressed in monetary terms and included in ROI only in the minority of cases where it has an immediate and direct impact on resource efficiency.

For another example, doing existing performance management processes more efficiently can save time and expenses, freeing up employees and managers to focus on organizational priorities. The monetary equivalent value of that time can be added to the conserved out-of-pocket expenses to calculate the ROI of the performance management process improvement. That is an efficiency calculation, a measure of time conserved by improving the process.

More important for strategy execution is whether the performance management system rewards and encourages the behaviors needed for the organization to succeed in the marketplace. A proper analysis of whether budget allocations support strategy execution depends first and foremost on whether that spending supports the organization's competitive advantage. Does the performance management system promote behaviors aligned with or opposed to the strategy? Are the expectations for role performance consistent with the talent available to staff the roles, both internally and externally? Those are the ultimate measures of strategic value added, not ROI produced through minimizing the cost of conducting the performance management processes.

ROI is not an effective tool for assessing the long-term benefit from improved HR processes and organizational effectiveness. A much better approach would specify how the HR program or human capital initiative supports building and maintaining the organizational capability needed for strategy execution. Applied the right way, the Strategic Analytics approach, using a causal model like the one shown in figure 5, can show that link (see chapter 7 for specific examples).

Other common measurements that fall short of what Strategic Analytics can do. A wide range of measurements and evaluation approaches are used in organizations today, aside from ROI. Any approach that does not include causal modeling is going to be deficient. Here I discuss three of them: revenue per employee, linkage analysis, and employee engagement. The critiques leveled here are just as applicable to the host of other measures that are in common use these days.

Revenue per employee. Revenue per employee is a proxy for high productivity and is easy to calculate. It is overly simplistic because it does not explain how the revenue is achieved, and it is the worst type of apples-to-oranges metric when revenues are compared across industries. Revenue per employee in capital-intensive industries, like oil and gas and aerospace, will always be higher than in service industries like retailing, hospitality (restaurants and hotels), consulting, and temporary staffing. Increases in productivity will increase revenue per employee in the service industries, but never to the point of getting it remotely close to the revenue per employee in the capital-intensive industries.

Even within the same industry, differences in the types of products and services provided can lead to different revenue per employee for many reasons other than productivity differences. For example, consider Microsoft and Google. Both are technology companies whose products are built on software, and they compete in most of the same markets. Despite those similarities, the source of each company's competitive advantage is very different. Microsoft's competitive advantage derives from dominating the market for operating systems for desktop and laptop computers. Google's competitive advantage comes from dominating the market for Internet search on those same computers.

For both companies, the biggest current threat is the move to mobile communications. Whether Microsoft or Google has higher revenue per employee is not relevant for understanding whether they will be successful at meeting this strategic threat. Both companies face the prospect of declining revenue per employee. In Microsoft's case, if revenue per employee declines because they stay primarily focused on desktop and laptop operating systems while that market shrinks, that would be a sign of strategic failure. If, in contrast, they succeed at building a successful business in the mobile space, the lower margins there would also almost certainly lead to falling revenue per employee, at least initially. In Google's case, even though it is developing a leading position in mobile Internet search that is similar to its lead in desktop and laptop Internet search, the lower margins available in mobile search are putting pressure on its profitability and revenue per employee. Thus Google's stock price has come under pressure even as it succeeds in moving to the mobile space.

The Microsoft and Google example illustrates why revenue per employee is not a useful metric for diagnosing strategy execution. Productivity is impacted by the discretion and decisions of the leaders and employees, as well as by external factors and shifts in the marketplace. Revenue per employee offers zero insight into how to improve strategy execution; there is no causal link from specific jobs or processes to increased revenue. For that we need a metric that focuses on measuring the impact of decisions and changes intended to improve strategy execution.

Linkage analysis. Linkage analysis has received a lot of attention in recent years. It offers the promise of demonstrating a connection between investments and process improvements on the one hand and operational metrics on the other hand. It consists of statistically estimating the relationship between changes in the investments or process improvements and changes in the operational metrics.

In its simplest form, linkage analysis connects measurements involving people (employee attitudes and capabilities) with business performance metrics. Within the scientific community there is considerable debate whether the positive statistical relationship measures true causation or just correlation. For example, those firms that are the most successful also have greater means to spend more lavishly on their employees—Google is the most prominent current example. A statistical link between HR interventions and business performance can exist even when the causation runs from business performance to HR spending, not vice versa.

Linkage analysis is appealing because you can always construct an argument for why the measurements involving people *should* matter for business performance. In many cases it is likely that the causation does run from spending on people and HR to positive business impacts. However, just because something *should* contribute to improved organizational effectiveness and performance, there typically is no guarantee that it *will*—and often many scenarios under which it won't. For example:

- Training plays an important role in closing competency gaps, so measures of training incidence should be correlated with improved performance; however, training is not the only contributor to improved performance and often is not the most important one (chapter 12).
- Measures of competency demonstration should also be correlated with improved performance, even though

some of the most important competencies that drive performance cannot be measured well and thus are missing from the set of measurements (chapter 10).

- Coaching is an important part of effective feedback and performance management, yet it is rarely cited as the most important or critical barrier to performance; instead, it is a contributor to improved performance while rarely, if ever, being "the" cause (chapter 7).

The problem is with linkage analysis that focuses on only one of the measures above. The analysis is highly likely to show a statistical correlation between the people measure and organizational effectiveness and performance. As the discussion above demonstrates, even though the correlation may be strong, it cannot be attributed to true causation.

Employee engagement. In my previous book, *Employee Surveys That Work*, I discussed in depth the relationship between employee engagement and business performance. Here I review and highlight some of the key issues and refer those interested in more details to my previous book.

The argument that employee engagement causes improved performance makes intuitive sense but does not necessarily hold empirically. The easiest way to make most employees happy is to keep their compensation the same and cut their responsibilities in half. However, doing so would completely destroy profits. Thus employee engagement does not always "cause" improved organizational performance.

Employee engagement and business results are statistically related because they are correlated, with the causation usually running the other way around: better business results lead to engagement, not vice versa. Even when you can show statistically that increased engagement in one year precedes increased business performance in the following year, as Harter, Schmidt, and Hayes (2002) showed using the Gallup data, that does not prove causation because both trend up together. When performance is going well, engagement tends to improve, which helps support further increases in business performance, and so on. The opposite also holds: falling business performance causes morale to drop, which hinders improvements in performance, which further hurts morale, and so on.

Consider a counterexample: when was the last time employee engagement scores fell in the year *before* business results deteriorated? If employee engagement is truly such a strong driver of business performance, we would have more documented cases than needed to fill up an encyclopedia. Instead, virtually every time business results fall first, and that drop causes morale to fall. People feel worse because the business is not achieving the goals established by the leaders. In addition, the organization stops doing all the "discretionary" things to boost employee morale. So you can't assume that changes in employee engagement necessarily predate changes in business performance.

In some settings more engaged employees can lead to increased sales and profitability. Employees in roles that have direct customer contact can affect how customers feel: engaged employees can induce customers to spend more or feel better about the customer service they receive, increasing customer retention (chapter 8). Even in organizations that rely on retail sales and customer service as core parts of their business model, only the employees in roles that interface directly with the customers can sway purchasing decisions with their own engagement. All the other roles in the organization contribute to organizational performance by doing their jobs, even if they are only "just satisfied" without being "highly engaged." Organizations often can staff back-office roles with less interpersonally positive and engaging people without hurting customer satisfaction because these roles are a step or two removed from the direct customer interface.

The usefulness of engagement measures is similar to a patient's temperature reading: if the patient's temperature deviates significantly from 98.6 degrees Fahrenheit, you can be sure something is happening that requires monitoring. In a similar way, measuring employee engagement can be important as a general gauge of business health: if engagement indices turn down, you can be sure that something is happening that needs to be addressed. However, a doctor would never fully diagnose an illness simply through taking the patient's temperature, and the same limitation applies to determining organizational interventions simply on the basis of employee engagement scores. In both cases additional information is needed to determine the true cause of the overall problems at hand; see chapter 8 for further discussion and details.

Summary. All of the measures discussed here fall short of telling a complete story that links people and business processes to improved strategy execution. ROI focuses too much on cash flow and not enough on organizational capability. Revenue per employee offers no insights into how specific jobs and processes contribute to competitive advantage. Linkage analysis and employee engagement are just as likely to identify correlations as causation.

A better approach to use is Strategic Analytics, which can tell the complete story if applied the right way. Part II provides the details.

Part II

How to Do Strategic Analytics

The seven chapters in this part of the book detail the "how to" steps in Strategic Analytics.

Chapter 3 provides tips and insights you need to know before getting started, including the right order for doing the analysis, the relationship with scorecards, the importance of conducting interviews and qualitative analysis, and who should construct the causal model.

Chapter 4 covers step 1 in the Strategic Analytics process. It provides a detailed discussion of how to identify the organizational strengths that define your competitive advantage and the weaknesses that threaten it. You start with identifying the sources of competitive advantage and focus the enterprise and human capital analysis on those.

Chapter 5 covers step 2 in the Strategic Analytics process—enterprise analytics. The focus includes deciding what part of the business you should focus on: the entire enterprise, a business unit, or a business process. The specific focus depends on the strategic outcomes you are trying to affect and whether the key activities take place across the whole organization or in one part.

Chapter 6 covers step 3 in the Strategic Analytics process—human capital analytics. Human capital analytics diagnose performance barriers and enablers at the role, individual, and/or HR process levels. The analytics focus on alignment and gaps in the job design, individual competencies, and motivation and attitudes.

Chapter 7 presents case studies of what the Strategic Analytics look like when you conduct a complete end-to-end analysis. It also shows how to use the framework to get to deeper insights even if you do only one or two of the steps. Chapters 8 and 9 provide details on specific applications of the Strategic Analytics approach, covering customer retention and profitable growth, and go-to-market strategies.

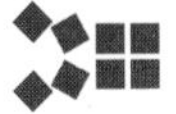

Chapter 3

Put the Horse in Front of the Cart—Where to Focus the Analysis

Issues Addressed in This Chapter

- Get the order right: competitive advantage analytics first, then enterprise analytics, and human capital analytics last.
- Enterprise analytics before human capital analytics so structural problems are addressed.
- Do analytics first to determine the right HR scorecard metrics.
- Always do stakeholder interviews and qualitative analysis.
- Advanced statistical analysis is not relevant for enterprise level and business unit level issues.

Key Questions

- How do key stakeholders see the strategy playing out in the organization design? Where do they see issues with strategy execution and where do they not?
- How to reconcile key stakeholders' views of strategy issues with each other?
- Are structural issues downplayed or ignored because they are too hard or too political to deal with?
- What new versus existing data do you need about people and processes to diagnose the strategy execution problems?

Before we dive into the specific steps involved in Strategic Analytics, this chapter first covers a number of issues you need to be aware of. Most important is the right order for analysis. It's also essential that you understand (a) how Strategic Analytics relate to scorecards, (b) where the data you will need comes from, (c) the importance of qualitative analysis, (d) who should build the causal model, and (e) the insights gained just from building the model even if you don't have enough time to test it rigorously.

Do enterprise analytics first to surface structural issues. Causal models in organizational analysis are not new. Understanding causation is a main motivation for using process improvement tools like Six Sigma, lean, and the approaches discussed in chapter 2. Those tools try to address the sources of waste, inefficiency, revenue loss, lack of employee engagement, and so on, but they don't necessarily include formal causal modelling. Even when they try to address causality, the focus typically is not on improvements in strategy execution. A more common focus is process improvements that can boost short-term cash flow but do not necessarily contribute to long-term competitive advantage. For that kind of impact, you must first identify which organizational capabilities are most important for strategic success and then focus the analysis on those capabilities.

You need to know the structural issues to avoid throwing good money after bad ideas. If the business has organizational design problems that should be fixed first, then that's what the decision makers should be told, even if they say they don't want to focus on structure. Delivering unwelcome news is better than chasing solutions that are doomed to fail because of unresolved structural issues. Sometimes the best course of action is to do nothing at all.

I say this based on decades of experience working with companies my colleagues and I have had at the Center for Effective Organizations. We have been approached for help so many times with an initial, narrowly-focused diagnosis of a company's motivation or skills/capabilities problem. A full systems diagnosis often reveals structural issues at the foundation of at least some of the problems. In many cases, if the organizational design issues aren't addressed, there is no guarantee of big improvements in performance and strategy execution.

For example, the compensation budget often is too low for a role. This leads to incumbents with skills gaps who can't perform at the expected level. This situation frequently is misdiagnosed as a motivation problem. Yet if the underlying compensation issue is not addressed, no amount of performance management will completely solve the challenges of attracting and retaining people with the right skills.

Similar kinds of structural issues often exist at the group/team, function, and business unit levels. Examples include:

- Decision rights aren't properly allocated, people overstep the appropriate boundaries, and cross-functional collaboration is undermined.
- A team's resource support falls short of its needs.
- The organization's culture is too conservative and inclusive. Decision making is needlessly drawn out to include everyone's voice.
- And so on.

There always are structural shortcomings that can be addressed. Any solution designed at the individual job level (such as better training, different recruitment methods, tweak incentive compensation, get leaders to be passionate, etc.) will stand a greater chance of being successful if it is aligned with the structural issues. That is the basis for ordering the analysis as indicated in figure 7.

Your chances of improving strategy execution are greatly enhanced if you first identify the structural factors that are potential barriers. For example, if decision rights aren't properly allocated, you can appeal to people's commitment to the organization and encourage them to do the right thing. But you'll continually run into conflicts that are created by the improperly defined decision rights. If you ignore problems with unclear decision rights, underinvestment in the compensation of a role,

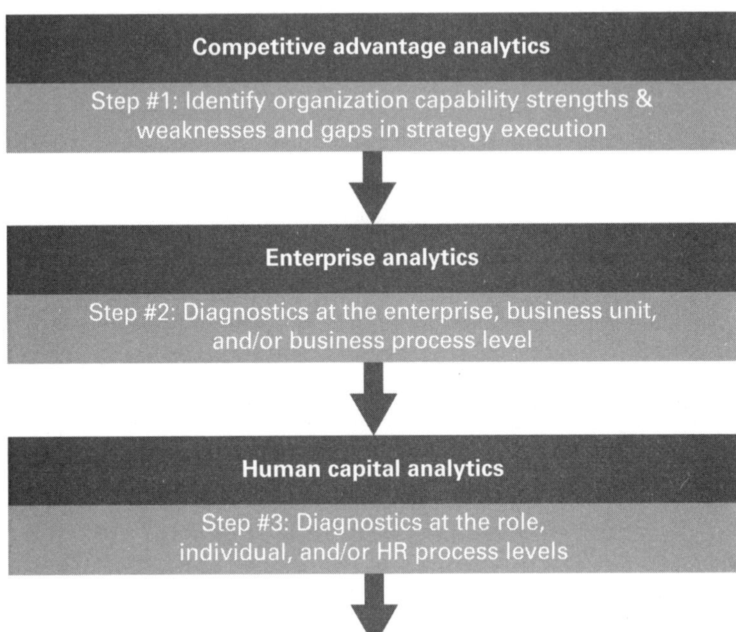

Figure 7: Strategic Analytics Roadmap

organization structures that are not aligned, and other fundamental issues, the best you can hope for is an imperfect resolution to problems with executing your strategy.

THE DANGERS OF A LITTLE DATA MINING

The motivation behind data mining is eminently reasonable: you look for statistically meaningful relationships between measures to inform further analysis. However, data mining is one of the most risky things you can do with HR data. If people are clamoring for insights and you find an interesting relationship in the data, it is tempting to present the results to engage your audience. But presenting interesting relationships is very different from specifying and testing a full causal model.

The risk is that if you show them a statistically significant relationship, they likely will assume something should be done. Action-oriented leaders, who are commonly found, often jump to designing solutions based on bits of data and preliminary but incomplete insights. They figure that doing something is better than doing nothing.

For example, suppose there is a positive correlation between performance ratings and people who are promoted from within, compared to people hired in from outside. A logical conclusion is that internal promotions are more productive. After one look at that simple analysis, an action-oriented leader might easily conclude that external hiring should be deemphasized. But further analysis might undermine or even contradict that conclusion.

Performance ratings can be biased by cultural fit. Internally promoted people may get higher ratings because they know how to act within the company culture, even if they aren't more productive. External hires also can have a harder time knowing where to go to get help. So they may indeed have lower performance, but not because they are incapable of performing—it's because they aren't properly supported by and integrated into the organization.

Both of these possible explanations are reasons why it is premature to jump to a solution like emphasizing internal promotions. First you need to establish the larger business need addressed by hiring externally. Fresh blood from outside may be critical for staying current on customer trends and your competitors' strategies. If those fresh faces get lower performance ratings because they challenge the dominant culture, that may be because they are doing exactly what you want them to do.

How does all this relate to balanced scorecards? Kaplan and Norton's balanced scorecard and strategy map tools (Kaplan and Norton 1996 and 2004) are a cornerstone of management practice. From the enterprise perspective, strategy maps are an excellent way of identifying the key business objectives and processes that the organization must execute in order to make the strategy successful. They are used to identify internal processes that drive strategic success, align investments in people and processes, and expose gaps in strategy execution. When done right, they provide the details on what needs to be done to maintain and build competitive advantage. Strategy maps can help focus attention on the customer value proposition and the key internal processes needed to deliver it.

The situation on the human capital side is not as positive. Though the balanced scorecard has become one of the most commonly used management tools for measuring and managing organizational performance and processes, Kaplan and Norton themselves acknowledge that the least well-developed quadrant deals with the human capital side:

> *[W]hen it comes to specific measures concerning employee skills, strategic information availability, and organizational alignment, companies have devoted virtually no effort for measuring either the outcomes or the drivers of these capabilities. This gap is disappointing since one of the most important goals for adopting the scorecard measurement and management framework is to promote the growth of individual and organizational capabilities .... Frequently, the advocates for employee training and reskilling, for employee empowerment, for information systems, and for motivating the work force take these programs as ends in themselves. The programs are justified as being inherently virtuous, but not as means to help the organization accomplish specific long-run economic and customer objectives.... This gap leads to frustration: senior executives wonder how long they are expected to continue to make heavy investments in employees and systems without measurable outcomes, while human resource and information system advocates wonder why their efforts are not considered more central and more strategic to the organization.* (1996, p. 144)

Though Kaplan and Norton's observation is two decades old, there has been little progress. More often than not, scorecards use the "best available" metrics, that is, the *least worst* of what is sitting around. There is little validation that these metrics can provide strategic insights.

THE DANGERS OF "INNOCUOUS" REPORTING, A.K.A. DOES TURNOVER BELONG IN SCORECARDS?

The balanced scorecard has popularized the idea that organizations should regularly measure and monitor key metrics about people. And if there are data available that describe what is going on with the people in your organization, what's the harm in reporting them? Isn't more information better than less?

The answer is "yes and no." Sticking your head in the sand and acting as if there are no data to inform human capital decisions ignores reality. But reporting HR data simply for the sake of sharing is not smart. If you present data without knowing its full value and how to act on it, you will create more problems than you solve. You need a model of what's driving the behavior you're observing and why you should care about it. HR scorecard data needs to be actionable and meaningful, not just available.

Consider turnover. What is the "right" level of turnover? In a call center, 50% annual turnover could be a cause for celebration, while 15% turnover for nuclear power plant engineers could be a disaster. The only way to tell the story the right way is to provide further information about the context. Many call centers have annual turnover in excess of 100%, so getting to 50% could be a great achievement. There are a very limited number of nuclear power plant engineers in most countries, so losing even one can create issues for the companies running these plants.

What about "regrettable" turnover, the label given to losing high performers? Don't you want that turnover as low as possible? Not necessarily. In order to attract high performers, you may have to offer them opportunities to contribute and grow, along with a clear path to moving on to bigger and better things elsewhere. If the cost of getting high performers to come work for you is that you will lose them in one or two years, then losing them could be a good thing. It's certainly better than not getting them in the first place. Lower turnover might be attainable only by hiring people with less ability to begin with, and then productivity and profits would suffer. What matters is not just the transaction costs of turnover (the costs of developing, retaining and replacing people in key positions), but also their contribution to productivity and strategy execution while they are working for you.

Treating scorecard data with CARE. The problem with scorecards is that they can be populated only with data that satisfy four criteria, summarized by the acronym CARE:

- Consistent: the data underlying the metric must be measured consistently over time
- Accurate: the data must be accurate, with few to no errors in recording it
- Reliable: the data must be a reliable proxy of what is supposed to be measured
- Efficient: the cost of collecting the data must be minimal

Relatively few human capital metrics fit the CARE criteria, which leaves organizations with few options for people metrics to populate scorecards. Too often the task is accomplished by turning to generic metrics like employee turnover, safety, the number or percentage of people completing training or developmental objectives, and so on. Those metrics *may* provide strategic insights in certain settings. However, the causal model first has to be specified and tested to ensure that these metrics are the correct focus.

For example, safety data are usually readily available. And we certainly want our employees to be safe. So why not populate a scorecard with safety data? If it's a manufacturing, construction, or mining operation, or some other type of work that involves heavy machinery and bodily risk, then safety is a very important metric. Putting it into a scorecard to hold managers accountable is a good idea. But be aware of these two caveats: (a) the metric is best used only in the parts of the organization where there is the greatest risk, and (b) even in those cases, it's not necessarily useful for improving strategy execution. Safety may be more of a status quo metric: you definitely want to maintain safe operations, but that may be irrelevant for improving margins, market share, customer retention, and so on. Is it useful for monitoring and holding managers accountable? Absolutely. Strategic? Not necessarily.

When you build and validate the causal model, you often identify measures that cannot be measured with CARE. This makes the task of creating meaningful scorecards much more difficult: most highly relevant human capital metrics cannot be collected systematically and accurately at low cost. After conducting a one-time analysis to identify the right metrics, use the results to make the business case for more systematic collection. Putting those metrics in your scorecards requires setting up measurement systems and processes so that they can be measured with CARE.

Just build it and you will gain insights. When you build the causal model from interviews with key stakeholders, you gain insights into key drivers of organizational performance. The stakeholders help you identify factors that are most likely to be important and exclude factors that have only a remote chance of making a difference.

For example, suppose you want to know the drivers of manufacturing efficiency. At the enterprise level, it is safe to exclude customer relationship management (CRM) systems as potential factors and to include inventory management systems. Inventory management systems are important for keeping inventory holding costs down while minimizing shortages, a key contributor to manufacturing efficiency. CRM systems, on the other hand, are important for customer retention but not really relevant for manufacturing efficiency.

On the human capital side, it is safe to include a role for skill-based compensation of manufacturing employees and to exclude the onboarding process of administrative assistants. Skill-based compensation has been shown to be an important contributor to building capabilities like manufacturing efficiency, so it is a good candidate for inclusion. Administrative assistants have a role to play; however, their role is too small to expect that improvements in their onboarding process will have any significant impact on manufacturing efficiency.

Building a causal model that is complete "enough" without being overly engineered or complicated means considering the range of potential enterprise and human capital factors without going overboard. If you are left with a large number of potential factors after going through the process of ruling factors in and out, you may need to go through another round that removes the least likely factors. There is no steadfast rule on the maximum number of factors to include in a causal model. However, if the list is greater than thirty or forty, the chances are extremely good that you can narrow it down without losing potential leading drivers of effective strategy execution. In many cases, you may have no more than ten or fifteen leading factors to consider by the time you have finished doing the model building.

The model building itself does not require a long time, though interviews with key stakeholders are needed to assess the importance of various factors. With focused efforts, those interviews usually can be conducted relatively quickly, over the course of a few weeks. Chapter 7 has examples of causal models.

The appendix has sample questions you can use as a template for the stakeholder interviews. If possible, the person or people who conduct the interviews should have experience. Conducting interviews the right way is essential to gathering the information needed for the diagnostic and model building. Interview training in social science methods is important but does not require formal qualifications. The skills can be accessed through books, training programs, and/or mentoring with experienced interviewers.[1]

Get alignment before starting the analysis. In order to maximize the chances that senior leaders will act based on your analysis, you have to get alignment up front on the need for the analytics. The initial stakeholder interviews serve a dual purpose: they gather information to diagnose what is going on with the system, and they engage those stakeholders in the process. Stakeholder engagement is essential for the work to have an impact for a number of reasons.

First, you need to get key decision makers on board regarding the need for the analysis. Even if they are already convinced of the need, letting them know that the analysis will happen is essential to ensure their support. For those who are supportive, the initial interviews can solicit their input on potential barriers you will encounter and ensure they buy into the process for collecting data and doing the analysis. For others who are skeptical about the work, interviews can help them to engage in the work or at least to keep them from erecting road blocks to doing the analysis.

Second, it is never too early to start thinking about using the analysis results to drive change. The case for change starts well before conducting analysis and writing reports. You need to have alignment on the potential need well before the analytics tell you what changes are in order. You start making the potential case for change when you define the issues to be addressed at the start of the work. Otherwise you run the risk that the results will be rejected because they weren't expected—even if they offer the most profound insights on improving strategy execution.

For example, in one case an HR analyst at a financial services firm found that an incentive pay plan was not driving the

[1]Weiss's (1995) book is a comprehensive treatment of the subject and a good place to start for anyone with no interview training or experience. Online resources can provide a starting point for learning but typically offer limited content. Articles such as Roulston, deMarrais, and Lewis (2003) cover details that can help someone who has a basic knowledge of interviewing techniques.

intended results. Rigorous analysis questioned a large number of assumptions about the pay plan and what drove behavior in the role. Yet the general manager responsible for that part of the business was not engaged in the investigative process from the beginning and was presented only with the final results at the end. As a result he totally rejected the findings and wouldn't listen to what the HR analyst had to say. The HR analyst's mistake was not engaging the general manager at the start of the process to ensure alignment on the need for the analysis and on the potential actions that would follow the findings (Levenson, 2011).

Data sources and biases (a.k.a. learning to love both interviews and surveys). Building the model is only part of the battle. Finding the right data to test it is just as important. And in some cases the precise data you need may be hard to obtain.

For example, it is well known that goal setting can impact organizational performance. If goals are set with appropriate "stretch" built into them—that is, relatively aggressive goals that are still achievable—they can serve as powerful motivators. However, if the goals are not humanly achievable, they can perversely demotivate people from being productive.

The challenge for the analysis is the difficulty in assessing goal-setting quality. It cannot reliably be measured by asking people about how hard their goals are. They have a strong incentive to report inaccurately that their goals are too difficult to achieve. So a self-reported survey measure of goal setting appropriateness is not reliable.

Does this mean that goal-setting quality should be left out of the causal model? Deciding which elements to include in the causal model based on what data are readily available is like putting the cart before the horse. If you want the truth about barriers to executing your strategy, you would never build a causal model based only on what sets of data are just sitting around. If goal setting is a critical potential factor, then you have to take the time and effort to decide how to measure it appropriately.

	Strength	Weakness
Operational and financial metrics	• Used by the business to determine strategy execution • No one questions usefulness	• Need full causal model to understand the link between people, processes, and business metrics
Existing employee archival data	• Objective measures of demographics, compensation, skills/ competencies, career paths, and other factors	• No insights into motivation • Can't answer why things happen the way they do
Existing survey and 360 data	• No additional cost to use the data • People familiar with the measures	• Not sufficiently comprehensive • Data not originally collected for the specific inquiry
New survey data	• Fill in the gaps in existing data • Inclusive process where everyone's voice is included	• Survey fatigue / time and cost to collect • Measuring for measurement's sake vs. as part of a change process
Interviews	• Tell the story of what is happening • Measure organizational alignment • Enable effective surveys	• Feasible only on small scale • May need survey for validation

Table 2: Sources of Data Used for Analysis

The different types of data that you can use for an analysis are described in table 2. The first three rows describe existing data: (a) operational and financial metrics, (b) employee archival data, and (c) survey data already collected. The last two rows describe new data: (d) new survey data, and (e) interviews.

The roles people have tend to push them toward favoring some types of data over others. Business leaders and operational managers tend to focus primarily on the objective data represented by the operational and financial metrics, and they supplement that with the "hard" data on employees that come out of the archival systems. They look at headcount ratios, average compensation, time needed to fill vacant roles, tenure, and similar metrics.

HR and organization development (OD) professionals tend to focus primarily on existing data from HR systems and on existing employee survey data. They look at measures like span of control, competency profiles, 360 ratings (where people are rated on observed behaviors by supervisors, peers, and direct reports), performance ratings, and attitudinal measures from existing employee surveys.

What tends to get de-emphasized by both business leaders and HR is collecting new data. The right column of table 2 shows the problem with taking that approach: weaknesses in existing data sources. These sources were rarely collected for your specific purpose, so almost always there are big gaps between what they measure and what you need. Consequently, there is no substitute for collecting new data through additional surveys, interviews, or both.

People who are data-driven decision makers gravitate toward surveys for new data collection. They like the quantifiable results and the large number of data points surveys can collect. People who are more process and interpersonally oriented gravitate toward stakeholder interviews for new data collection. They like to tell the story about what is happening. Surveys and interviews are complementary. If you have the time and resources, you likely will want to do both. But surveys take a back seat to interviews. You always start with interviews, which often are all you need. There might be no justification for a survey.

Choose qualitative analysis over quantitative to start. The initial information to be collected for a diagnostic has to include interviews of key informants. Data from prior analyses can always be included as well: where sales or customer service are falling short of goals, where productivity is low, where operations are inefficient, and so on. But there is no way to avoid interviews. They are a critical part of initial information gathering.

If you're trying to understand a thorny organizational issue where lots of different roles, functions, or work groups are involved; where people have competing agendas they are trying to accomplish; or where you just want to understand deeply why things are happening the way they are, you have to start with interviews. The interviews should include people at the center of the issue (the people in the roles doing the core work), their supervisors and leaders higher up, their direct reports, people who work with them in support or coordinating roles (who contribute to or receive the output from the work), and other informed people in the organization who have a good perspective on the dynamics involved.

Interviews are the best way to narrow down the scope of likely causal factors. You can't design and field a survey that is comprehensive enough to address all potential issues. A survey that comprehensive would have hundreds of questions. Surveys are like one-way conversations. The "virtual" interviewer (survey administrator) has to commit to everything asked up front because there is no way to follow up based on the interviewees' (the survey respondents') answers. Interviews are much more effective for initial exploration of the issues at hand.

You can use interviews to collect survey-type data. Many surveys of consumer and worker behavior are administered by trained interviewers who collect the information verbally and record it on computers so the respondents don't have to enter it themselves. I once evaluated in-store performance for a large consumer products company where I administered the survey verbally and recorded the answers myself. The data can then be tabulated just as if they had been collected via a traditional survey. In addition, open-ended interview responses can be coded using text analysis, quantifying the frequency that particular themes are mentioned.

In another example, I coled an evaluation of the effectiveness of customer teams for a large multinational company. The teams were responsible for interfacing with the company's biggest customers and drew members from the different business units (major product lines) and functions (manufacturing, marketing, sales and distribution, and so on). Our objective was to understand how well the teams were coordinating their work and meeting both the customers' and the company's needs for product mix, price, service, and promotions.

We used an interview-only approach for the diagnostics for two reasons. First, though the nominal structure of each team was the same (with the same roles), each team was staffed with different people and had different customer needs. Consequently, the dynamics on each team were unique, including the personalities and client-induced mandates. We needed the richness of interviews to get into all the nuances driving behavior on each of the teams.

Second, even if we wanted to we could not have conducted a statistical analysis of differences across the groups. There were fewer than fifteen teams, so we had to use a form of case study analysis. (See the discussion below about the minimum sample size required for statistical analysis). We used the interviews to probe about the same set of issues across all teams and looked for commonalities and differences across them. The types of factors we considered included (a) resource support provided to the teams, (b) their degree of autonomy in making customer-specific exceptions to corporate pricing and product mix rules, (c) the incentives and rewards team members received for being on the teams, (d) points of tension and alignment between the teams and the business units and functions, (e) how serving on the teams fit into key individuals' career paths, and more. We used the results of the interview analysis to recommend changes to improve the teams' effectiveness.

Who should build the causal model? Learning how to build causal models can be an important skill whether you manage the business or support it. This is not a requirement for people in a number of frontline roles and their immediate supervisors. Yet for many other people, knowing how certain tasks contribute more to organizational success than others can guide them to be more effective. Building the causal model—or at least being aware of the issues involved—enables them to see how their piece of the puzzle contributes to strategy execution.

If you want to understand, influence and manage how the organization reacts to the causal model and analysis results, you should never fully relinquish the task of model building to anyone else in the organization. There are specialists for whom building and testing models is a job requirement; this group includes people with roles in strategy and analytics. While they may take the lead, you still can engage directly in the model building process. That will ensure you have the deepest understanding of what drives strategy execution. You also can make sure key factors have not been excluded inadvertently. Not everyone has to spend a large amount of time on it—you don't want too many cooks in the kitchen. But you nonetheless need people to be connected so they can learn from the process and guide it, if it is appropriate that their input be considered.

Where to apply statistics for testing the model. One final point about testing causal models. Applying statistics to learn about data is analysis, but not all analysis requires statistical calculations like correlations, regression, and so on. In fact, for most analyses at the enterprise and business unit levels, it is impossible to apply statistical analyses like correlations and regression because there isn't enough data. Robust statistical analysis requires many examples (observations) of the thing you are analyzing, with enough common characteristics that you are comparing apples to apples. The general rule is that you need at least twenty-five to thirty of those similar things for statistical analysis. For a multivariate analysis like regression or anova, where you test the importance of a number of competing factors, the minimum number of observations can be fifty or even much higher.

A role with a large number of incumbents, say one hundred or more people, has more than enough to warrant statistical analysis including methods such as regression. If you examine business units or locations, you can apply statistical analysis if the units do the same thing; examples include retail outlets, manufacturing sites producing the same products, and call centers handling the same type of clients. If you are diagnosing issues at the enterprise level, however, there is only one unique observation, so no statistics can be applied.

Case study analysis can yield actionable insights even when you can't apply statistics. Case study analysis in this context means in-depth examination of the system, looking at the component parts to determine how they fit together and where improvements need to be made. It can be conducted quite rigorously at the enterprise level or when examining dissimilar business units or teams.

For the causal model in figure 5, the type of analysis to use depends on which part you are analyzing. For the top level, where measurements are at the role and individual worker level, analysis of behaviors (job performance, competencies, and similar areas) or attitudes (intention to leave, commitment, and so on) among a group of similar employees would use multivariate statistics. Analysis of job design, in contrast, requires a case study approach: even if a role has hundreds or even thousands of incumbents, there is only one job. Analysis of individual capability often uses univariate statistics (mean, median, minimum, maximum, range, frequency, and so on) and sometimes multivariate statistics (correlations, cross-tabulations, regression, anova, and so on).

The bottom part of the causal model in figure 5, the group or organizational level, also requires a mix of different types of statistical versus case study analysis. If you are examining multiple groups or sites that are similar, then you can apply multivariate statistics to determine the drivers of behaviors and performance. If the groups or sites are dissimilar or if you are focusing on business units or the enterprise, then you have to use case study analysis.

One more note about the appropriate use of statistical analysis. There are many instances in which data are collected for managers, including competency model data, which could be analyzed using multivariate statistics: the data represent common measures for a group of people doing the same set of management tasks. Yet these data typically cannot provide meaningful insights on strategy execution. That's because managers' roles in strategy execution vary greatly, depending on what part of the organization they are in and the processes they manage.

Managerial competency models are built to capture the commonalities across all managerial jobs; by necessity they ignore context-specific information. However, it's the context that is critical for deep insights into the drivers of performance for any one manager's group of direct reports. Managerial competency models are reduced to measuring the most common, least differentiated tasks that managers do across very different settings. You can do multivariate analysis of managerial competency data, but what you learn will likely be of little help in improving managerial performance. The competency data are ill-suited to explain the true drivers of managerial performance.

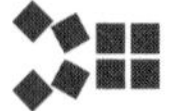

Chapter 4

Step 1—Competitive Advantage Analytics

Issues Addressed in This Chapter

- Step 1 in Strategic Analytics: Focus on the organizational capabilities that support competitive advantage and strategy execution gaps
- Competitive advantage is supported by high performance work design and is derived from some parts of your organization, not all
- Align high performance work design with the compensation philosophy

Key Questions

- What roles and business processes contribute to building and maintaining competitive advantage?
- Where do organizational capability weaknesses provide room for competitors to encroach?

- Are we trying to save money in the wrong places by cutting back on compensation where we need high performance?
- Do the HR metrics help contribute to competitive advantage?

Step 1 in Strategic Analytics is identifying the sources of your organization's competitive advantage. How does each role contribute and in what ways? Which roles and processes are more central for competitive advantage? You need the answers to these questions to evaluate if resources are being spent properly and whether performance expectations align with the organizational design.

There is no free lunch when it comes to designing an organization to support competitive advantage. If you need to increase investment in one area, the money has to come from somewhere. People have very different roles, and the contribution of those roles to creating competitive advantage varies tremendously. Even people working in the same type of job can contribute to the execution of your strategy in very different ways, if they work with different customers or business processes. The only way you can determine which parts of the organization, which roles, and which people in the roles have the potential to contribute more is by dissecting the sources of your competitive advantage.

How to avoid boiling the ocean. The causal chain from individual performance to group performance and, ultimately, business results is shown in figure 8, which is a simplified version of the causal model in figure 5 (chapter 1). Fixing problems at the people and process level *should* contribute to improved strategy execution and business results. Every day in organizations around the world, people start with the pieces that don't work and try to fix them because they *should* help improve business results.

The problem is the large gap between *should* and *will* when it comes to improving strategy execution and business results.

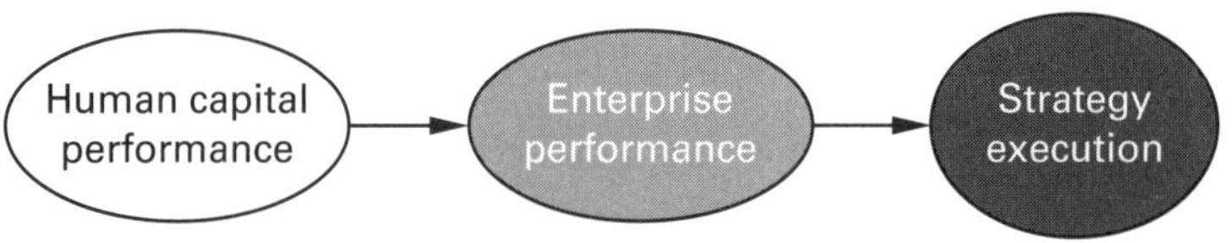

Figure 8: The Path from Individual to Team Contribution and Business Results

Organizations are extremely complex, with so many people, processes, and moving parts. Often a thousand things can be done to improve morale, engagement, skill development, career opportunities, communication, information sharing, and so on. Where is the solid evidence that a particular solution will improve strategy execution and the bottom line? If there is no clear link, I call those "nice-to-have" solutions, not "strategically important" solutions.

There are so many problems in organizations that would be nice to solve, you could spend your entire career addressing them without ever significantly improving strategy execution. If organizations had unlimited resources, my critique probably wouldn't matter. One army of people could focus on fixing the thousand "nice-to-have" things, while a second army focuses on improving strategy execution. However, we live in a world of limited time and resources. Do we want better employee morale? Absolutely. Should our people have better opportunities to learn and grow their skills on the job? Of course. Do we need to improve the quality of communication and information sharing within the organization? That's a no brainer. And so on. But we can't do *everything*. We have to prioritize, focusing on where our strategy execution falls short.

Fine tuning operations versus filling the gaps in strategy execution. There is an important distinction between work that ensures continuity of operations versus work that improves strategy execution. The overwhelming majority of activity in the business and in HR ensures continuity of what the business is currently doing. Improving those processes may not have any big upside for the bottom line. Despite that, the processes are very important for generating cash flow and profit—if the company stopped doing them, it would have big problems making money.

For example, on the people side hiring processes are critical so that vacancies are filled quickly. Compensation and benefits processes ensure people are paid the right amount on time and that benefits are appropriate. Performance management provides feedback so people can learn from their mistakes and be rewarded for doing their jobs well. And so on. If HR stopped doing this work, organizational effectiveness and business results would surely suffer.

On the business side, regional offices, manufacturing plants, retail outlets, distribution centers, R&D facilities, call centers, corporate headquarters, and more have to be managed every day, often 24x7. Leaders and frontline managers oversee operations to ensure that the business makes money and returns value to shareholders.

Tons of analytics are applied to understanding and optimizing everyday business and HR processes like these. However, as critical as these processes are, incrementally improving them is usually fundamentally different than changes that increase strategy execution where it's most needed. For example, servicing existing accounts and customers maintains operations without improving strategy execution. In contrast, increasing the rate of innovation, market share, and customer retention all are examples of strategy execution improvements, which are different than incremental improvements to existing processes.

ARE YOU HELPING TO IMPROVE STRATEGY EXECUTION WHERE IT'S MOST NEEDED?

There are a thousand things that can be done to fix existing processes and to help people do their jobs better and be more efficient. Managers can give better feedback and help their teams to do their work more efficiently. Manufacturing processes can be tweaked to reduce waste. Call centers can improve the volume of calls processed per hour to reduce wait times. Procurement can get better prices for raw materials, supplies, and business services. HR can improve the efficiency and effectiveness of recruiting, onboarding, and training. And so on.

Every single process improvement contributes to organizational success one way or another. But they also have an opportunity cost. There are big gaps in strategy execution that get too little attention when everyone focuses only on making incremental improvements in what they are already doing.

The key is to start with the greatest needs for improved strategy. Is it better customer retention? Improved innovation? Increased market share? These challenges keep your senior leaders up at night precisely because they don't receive enough attention. You should constantly ask yourself, "How is what I'm doing helping to move the needle on those gaps? What is the direct line of sight between what I'm doing and those outcomes?"

People often focus too much on incremental improvements because of the risk-reward tradeoff. If you can make a certain incremental improvement to existing processes, you can demonstrate a direct (and certain) impact of your decisions on the organization's bottom line. That helps both the organization and your performance rating in a low-risk way. Improving strategy execution where it's most needed promises a greater return to the bottom line, but with a much less certain chance of success. Many people are risk averse; if left to their own devices to decide where to focus their efforts to improve performance, they choose the easier route of incremental improvements to existing processes. This is one reason why there often is not enough attention paid to improving strategy execution where it's most needed.

Articulate your organizational strengths and weaknesses. In order for a solution to improve strategy execution where it's most needed, it has to address one of two needs: (a) bolstering the strengths that create competitive advantage for the organization or (b) shoring up weaknesses that expose the organization to competitive threats. In some cases the weaknesses are just mirror images of the strengths, but not always. The place to start is the strategy.

The basic question that defines strategy is "How do we develop and maintain our competitive advantage that enables us to make money where our competitors don't?" For example, Apple's strategy is to create unique, seamless user experiences with technology that surpasses what's available on the mass market—technology for which people will pay premium prices. Apple's weakness is innovation in lower-priced products that competitors offer with features that are "good enough" to attract consumers who would otherwise buy Apple's products. The organizational capabilities that Apple uses to defend its competitive advantage are innovation, marketing, and customer support. Any analysis that is going to help improve Apple's strategy execution needs to provide insights on bolstering its competitive advantage in those three capabilities.

For another example, the strategy of a health care organization, like a hospital or a physicians' group, is to provide high-quality care at a price point that keeps patients coming back. A weakness is lack of coordination across organizations in the health care system and a loss of focus on overall patient well-being. The organizational capabilities that are key to competitive advantage include the technical knowledge of patient treatment, ties to other doctors and health care providers for referrals, and patient interaction competencies (also known as bedside manner).

Start with your competitive advantage. Some parts of your organization and certain processes are more critical for competitive advantage than others. Which ones matter most and in what ways depends entirely on the specifics of your strategy and organization design.

The sources of your organization's competitive advantage often are different from the strategic objectives. Increasing market share is a strategic goal, not a strategy: the strategy is how market share is increased. Increasing sales or total profit by 10 percent isn't even a strategic goal, but just an operational goal. In order to achieve the operational goal, you need to focus on the capabilities that enable the organization to make money and in a way that is as good or better than your competitors.

Competitive advantage comes from the organizational capabilities that enable strategic goals to be reached. For example, for consumer products companies these are typically marketing (brand strength) and distribution (efficiency and effectiveness of go-to-market operations, measured in part by market share). For technology and engineering companies, a typical strength is technical excellence (quality, cutting edge technical features, and so on.). For telecommunications companies, the strength is a robust network that delivers high-quality, uninterrupted service.

Organization design imperfections and cross-functional integration challenges ensure that always there is room to improve the organizational capabilities that support competitive advantage. Every company has room to improve on their strengths to deliver even better marketing and distribution, technical excellence or network robustness, thereby enhancing strategy execution.

The weaknesses that pose a threat are the secondary organizational capabilities that correspond to the "weak underbelly" created by organizing around the primary organizational capabilities. These are the underdeveloped capabilities that, if successfully addressed, would enable the organization to be truly ambidextrous or agile.

In the case of consumer products companies, these weaknesses include the ability to develop and successfully grow new products without requiring that they immediately have a dominant market share. In the case of technology and engineering companies, it's building products with an equal emphasis on the customer experience and not just technical features. For telecommunications companies, it's innovating and incorporating features that delight customers at the risk of cannibalizing existing cash cow revenue streams, and doing so before competitors move first. Understanding your organization's competitive advantage strengths and weaknesses is a core element of analyzing the sources of strategy execution success and failure.

What to focus on depends on where you are in the organization. Regardless of the industry you're in and your organization's size, you have to start with your strategy to know where to focus the analytics. And if you're looking within a large organization at one part—a division, site, function, etc.—you need to make a clear link between what's happening there and the organization's overall strategy. Only with that knowledge in hand can you know what needs to be improved to support the organization's overall competitive advantage.

If your domain is a smaller part of a business unit—a site, department, team, etc.—you don't have the same options to think about redesigning entire organizational structures the way the business unit leaders do. But that doesn't mean you can ignore the importance of the overall strategy and structure of your organization. It is only through understanding the entire system—how everything works together—that you can know the role that specific processes and people play in improving strategy execution and how your part of the organization fits into the larger whole.

Large, multidivisional companies often have different strategies for each business unit that are distinct but may also be tied into each other. Disney's ESPN has a strategy of providing sports programming that is in high demand and can't be watched elsewhere. Its theme parks' strategy is to provide a magical immersive experience that can't be found anywhere else. The company's movie division focuses on story telling based on computer-animated fantasy (Pixar) and traditional animation and on live-action superheroes (Marvel) and science fiction (Star Wars). The movies are supposed to make money at the box office on their own. In addition, the child-oriented movies are supposed to tie into merchandising in its consumer products division and storytelling at the theme parks. The sources of competitive advantage in each part of Disney vary along with the strategy for each business unit.

Similar diversified stories can be told for companies like General Electric and for many of the conglomerates that dominate in countries like Japan, Korea, India, and Indonesia. Even when a multidivisional company is focused in one industry, like financial services or technology, different strategies drive the organizational structure and bottom-line results for different divisions. Citibank's strategies for making money in retail banking, commercial banking, and investment banking

Organization process	Industry				
	Biotech & Pharma	Technology	Consumer products & food	Aerospace	Professional Services & Consulting
R&D	Yes	Yes	No	Yes	No
Quality / operations	Yes	No	No	*Product dependent*	Market segment dependent
Branding / marketing	Yes	*Product dependent*	Yes	No	No
Distribution	No	*Product dependent*	Yes	No	Yes
Government Relations	Yes	No *(except for new market access)*	No *(except for new market access)*	Yes	No *(except for new market access)*
Customer service	No	*Product dependent*	No	No	Yes

Table 3: Sources of Competitive Advantage by Industry and Organization Process

are very different. IBM's strategies for making money in mainframe computers versus business services are quite separate and distinct. And so on.

Where competitive advantage resides in your organization. The first step to set up Strategic Analytics the right way is to identify where the capabilities that create competitive advantage reside in your organization. Consider the examples in table 3.

The rows in table 3 list key processes found in most organizations; the columns correspond to different industries. The entries in each cell indicate which processes are sources of competitive advantage for each industry. If you work in any of these industries or know them well, you can quibble with how I've characterized which processes are sources of competitive advantage. The point of table 1 is not to provide a definitive statement of the sources of competitive advantage for any single company in these industries—it's not meant as an investment guide. Instead, the point is to highlight basic patterns that are true across most companies in an industry.

Consider biotech and pharmaceuticals, for example. In this industry, R&D, manufacturing quality, branding, and government relations are all sources of competitive advantage:

- R&D is the source of new drugs that are covered under patent protection and the foundation of all profits in the industry.
- Manufacturing quality is critical to ensure drug safety and reliability, without which companies would be subject to enormous lawsuits and government fines.
- Branding and marketing are important to convince doctors to prescribe and patients to pay top dollar for drugs under patent protection when cheaper generic alternatives may be available.
- Government relations are critical to ensure compliance with regulation and approval to sell new drugs.

In contrast, distribution and customer service in this industry are not sources of competitive advantage:

- Distribution is important for keeping products stocked at pharmacies but is not responsible for driving incremental sales volume. Distribution is also not a key source of profits when selling branded drugs under patent protection with very high margins.
- Customer service is not a source of competitive advantage because doctors and patients do not choose drugs on that basis.

For an example that contrasts with biotech and pharmaceuticals, consider the consumer products industry, especially the large food companies that dominate national markets. These companies derive their competitive advantage primarily from branding/marketing and distribution: these are the critical organizational capabilities that enable them to maintain dominant market shares. Each company has an R&D department, but the products they turn out internally tend to be incremental innovations on existing product lines. The truly innovative new products tend to be invented at small companies that can grow a new product on a small scale but cannot compete with the large companies' marketing prowess and the scale and breadth of their distribution systems. So unless the small company that invented a new product wants to remain a niche player with limited national sales, it usually sells the product line to or is acquired by one of the large companies.

Work design and competitive advantage. The examples in table 3 demonstrate a universal fact: competitive advantage for any company is derived from some organizational processes but not all. The parts of the organization that more directly contribute to competitive advantage usually receive extra attention and investment: that is where it is most critical for the organization to perform as flawlessly as possible. Other parts of the organization usually get disproportionate responsibility for minimizing costs.

The structure of the team or job itself can directly impact performance. For many jobs and teams a range of job design options are available, with more narrowly defined jobs at one end, and more broadly defined, enriched jobs that require higher skill levels at the other end (chapter 10). What works best depends to a large extent on the context, the leaders' and supervisors' ability to manage the different types of work, the skills of the incumbent employees, and more.

When analyzing the sources of strategy execution success and failure, it is important to keep in mind the sources of competitive advantage and how decisions over which organizational capabilities to invest in are made. Budget constraints require all organizations to make hard choices about which capabilities will get proportionately greater investment and what the expectations for performance are from that extra investment. A key question for all organizational processes is whether the investment dedicated to that process is enough to support successful strategy execution. Yet "enough" means different things depending on whether the expectations are for high performance versus average performance for that process.

THE COMPETING SOURCES OF COMPETITIVE ADVANTAGE

In all industries, competitive advantage is created by emphasizing capabilities that strengthen the organization's market position and by shoring up weaknesses that hurt its market position. And those strengths and weaknesses often are two parts of the same whole: the weaknesses are created in the wake of organization design decisions that are supposed to build on the strengths.

Consider the case of consumer products companies like Nestle, Unilever, Proctor & Gamble, or others. Their competitive strengths are branding and marketing, along with the scale and efficiency of their distribution systems. Their weakness is breakthrough innovation, caused by specific features of their organizational design. They make money by producing and selling high volumes of products that are moved through their go-to-market systems quickly and efficiently (chapter 9). Incremental innovations (such as a new flavor of toothpaste, tea, or chocolate) are easy to test and deploy because they can be easily slotted into existing production equipment and distribution systems. But breakthrough innovation, such as the creation of an entirely new product line, runs into the chicken-versus-egg challenge of justifying the economics.

Unless it can be proven that a new product line will have a large enough customer base to realize economies of scale in production and distribution, the large consumer products companies typically won't take the risk on the new product. Instead, breakthrough innovations typically come from smaller companies. Once the small companies have shown that a market exists for a new product line, they sell their new product to or are acquired by the large firms. They do this because they cannot match the large firms' distribution systems, and creating one from scratch is prohibitively expensive.

Or consider the case of health care organizations with competing objectives of profitable operations and patient wellness. Many health care delivery organizations are partnerships or nonprofits to reduce the tension between the business side and patient wellness side, but that only relieves part of the pressure. It takes shareholders out of the equation who might force too heavy a focus on maximizing profits over patient wellness. That's important when there are longer-term impacts on patient wellness that aren't the responsibility of the current treating physician. But the organization still has to make enough money to cover operations and generate enough excess cash to deal with variability in accounts receivable from patient payments and insurance reimbursements. So the tension between making money and patient wellness persists.

Chapter 5

Step 2—Enterprise Analytics

Issues Addressed in This Chapter

- Step 2 in Strategic Analytics: How to conduct diagnostics at the enterprise, business unit, and/or business process levels
- Conducting qualitative analysis of organizational design and culture
- Organization design diagnostics: decision rights and dispute resolution
- Organization capability diagnostics: interdependencies and integration of tasks across roles
- Culture diagnostics: group norms aligned with strategic priorities
- Aligning resource allocation with strategic priorities

Key Questions

- How effectively does the organization's design support the desired capabilities that promote its competitive advantage?
- Where do breakdowns in communication and collaboration occur?
- Where does the culture enhance the organization's ability to execute the strategy, and where does it get in the way?
- Does resource allocation support strategy execution?

Chapter 4 described the first step in doing Strategic Analytics. In this chapter we address the second step: enterprise analytics. The three parts of enterprise analytics are in the bottom part of figure 5 (chapter 1) and are repeated here in figure 9:

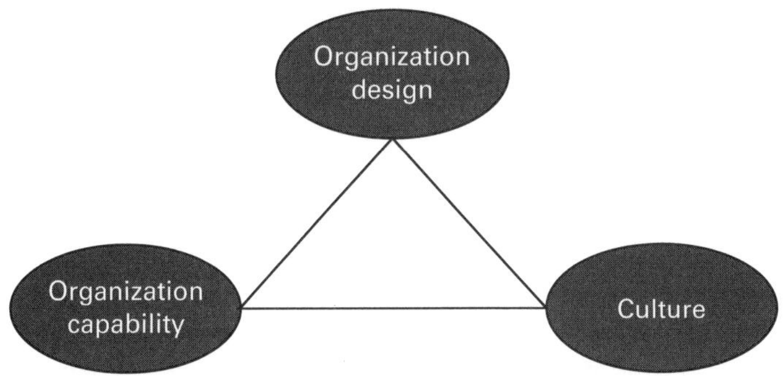

Figure 9: Enterprise Analytics Components

In this second step of Strategic Analytics, you diagnose each of the three components of enterprise analytics: the organization's design, capability, and culture. Addressing only one or two of the three components is not enough to ensure a robust diagnostic. With those results in hand, either you will be able to take action at that point, or you will be ready to conduct human capital analytics (chapter 6) to complete the Strategic Analytics diagnostic.

Organizational capabilities describe what parts need to be built to accomplish the strategy. Organization design describes the formal organization (the organizational chart) and the lateral structures and processes needed to get the work done. Culture and group norms describe how the work gets done. All three are needed to paint the full picture of the reasons for strategy execution success versus failure.

In many cases senior leaders are aware that all three have to be addressed, but they don't necessarily support a complete diagnostic. Organizational design and decision rights are a politically sensitive topic, so most people would prefer ignoring any structural problems rather than diagnosing them. The point of the diagnostic is *not* necessarily to redesign or even to make changes. Rather, because so many strategy execution problems arise from flaws in the organization's design, you need to understand what those flaws are and why they exist. If the changes you implement ignore the organization's design flaws, you almost certainly will fall short of the desired outcomes.

The organizational design diagnostics look for problems with the design decisions and lateral integration. How are decision rights allocated? Where do problems arise in decision making? How do people overcome the flaws in the organization's design? Where does matrix decision making need to be improved? Are resources properly allocated to support the strategy?

The second part of enterprise analytics, organizational capabilities diagnostics, focuses on the workflow and interdependencies among roles. What work has to be done to execute the strategy, to produce the organization's products and services? Who has to do what? How much integration versus differentiation among roles is needed?

The third part is culture diagnostics. Culture and group norms describe the idiosyncrasies that make working at each organization unique. Which aspects of the organization's design and capabilities reinforce the culture and make change more difficult? What are the group norms that drive behavior? Where do those group norms support effective strategy execution and where do they get in the way?

This chapter addresses each of those diagnostics in turn, providing key questions to address in each case. The chapter also includes the first part of the discussion on using high-involvement, high-performance work design to diagnose whether senior leaders have unrealistic expectations about productivity and quality goals. Self-managing work teams are covered here, while high-performance job design and compensation design are addressed in chapter 6. Chapter 10 presents a systematic treatment of high-performance work design and the identification of critical roles and talent.

The best way to use this chapter is as follows. The first time through you should read the entire chapter. Each section raises specific questions that you should know the answer to when doing a complete Strategic Analytics diagnostic. So you need to be familiar with the questions and issues that commonly need to be addressed. However, you do *not* need to do an in-depth analysis of every single issue when doing the work in practice. To the contrary, I have *never* been in a situation where a deep dive into all topics is needed. That's the point of conducting the initial stakeholder interviews—to determine the more likely sources of strategy execution problems and then focus the analysis (and any subsequent interviews) on those.

The key questions posed at the beginning of each section can be used as a launch point for designing an interview protocol for conducting those stakeholder interviews. The details within each section provide guidance for how to probe deeper on any issue that emerges as a more likely cause for which you need additional details for a complete diagnostic. The appendix provides an interview template that incorporates the enterprise diagnostic questions from this chapter and the human capital diagnostic questions from chapter 6.

KEY ORGANIZATIONAL DESIGN QUESTIONS

- How are decision rights allocated?
- Where do problems arise in decision making?
- How do people overcome the flaws in the organization design?
- Are there clear accountabilities that link the unit or team's objectives back to the strategy?
- Would reconfiguring the team to be more autonomous and self-managing increase engagement and productivity?

Organization Design Analytics

The primary issue to be addressed by organization design analytics is whether there is sufficient alignment between the strategy and the organization's design. Are each function's objectives sufficiently aligned with its structure—has it been set up the right way to get the work done? Are resources appropriately allocated across the organization to provide the support needed to get the work done? Have managers' and senior leaders' objectives been sufficiently defined, and are they held accountable for leading their teams and supporting the work of the enterprise? How much cross-functional collaboration is needed for enterprise success? Are people rewarded for focusing only on their functional silo and its issues, or for taking actions to support the strategy, even if the function's decision-making authority is undermined? Specific questions to address follow.

How are decision rights allocated? Where do problems arise in decision making? A key issue in organizational design is determining where primary decision rights reside. In most organizations, primary decision rights are assigned to the parts of the organization that provide the core of competitive advantage. For example, in pharmaceuticals it's R&D, while in consumer products it's marketing plus sales and distribution.

As soon as the primary decision rights are set, the problem arises of getting people to work together across organizational boundaries. The other parts of the organization have control over issues that fall solely under their domain, but those are usually only a small portion of the issues. For everything else, coordination with the primary decision rights holders in other parts of the organization is essential.

Problems of silo behavior are inherent in any organizational design. Assigning decision rights always creates coordination problems: (a) across different decision rights owners, (b) between those who have the information necessary for decision making and the decision makers, and (c) between people in parts of the organization with different reporting relationships (reporting up to different decision makers).

How do people overcome the flaws in the organization design? Do clear accountabilities link the unit or team's objectives back to the strategy? The main objective of organization design analytics is to determine where improvements are needed in matrix and cross-functional, cross-business-unit decision making. Use the stakeholder interviews to determine if the organization is overcoming the natural tendency toward silo behaviors. Are conflicts resolved efficiently with minimal time and resources wasted? Where does collaboration need to improve, to be more proactive, in order to achieve better strategy execution?

The formal statement of decision rights is one thing. Enforcement (encouragement, cajoling, or similar actions) of aligned behaviors is another matter entirely, especially for people and processes that are multiple levels below the senior leadership team. When you do the organizational design diagnostics, a key is to make sure people are held accountable and rewarded for doing the right thing for the organization, no matter where they are in the hierarchy. Are they rewarded for taking actions to improve strategy execution even in cases where their group or function's narrow self-interests may be undermined? Are middle managers and senior leaders held accountable for ensuring their actions support the strategic objectives of the entire organization?

Would reconfiguring the team to be more autonomous and self-managing increase engagement and productivity? A key issue in organizational design is the extent to which decision making is embedded lower versus higher in the hierarchy. The traditional command-and-control approach minimizes frontline decision making, at a cost of needing greater management oversight. The high-involvement, high-performance approach pushes decision making down to the frontlines, where possible, thus enabling less management oversight, greater managerial spans of control, and fewer managers. The end result can be greater productivity and higher quality.

Earlier in this chapter I argued that you want to do organizational design diagnostics even if you don't have permission to change the organizational design, so you can properly determine if structural factors are impeding productivity and strategy execution. A similar argument applies to assessing whether a team or business unit would benefit from a more high-involvement, high-performance work design. It may be hard to achieve the organization's or unit's productivity and quality goals under a more traditional, command-and-control design. Assessing the relevance of the high-performance, high-involvement approach can provide critical insights into whether senior leaders have properly designed and resourced the organization.

The history of and writing on high-involvement, high-performance work design is quite extensive. It starts with the innovations in manufacturing conceived by Edward Deming and pioneered by the Japanese automobile manufacturers half a century ago. It is now extensively used in manufacturing environments, and the principles apply to work in many other industries, products, and services. Here I will not provide an extensive review of everything that has been written about it—that would take an entire book of its own. Instead I provide key details that are relevant for Strategic Analytics diagnostics. We start here with a brief discussion of self-managing team design. Greater details are provided in chapter 6 around job design, with additional principles and details in chapter 10, including aligning compensation with the work design.

The principle behind high-involvement, high-performance design is that you can achieve greater productivity and quality in your operations through restructuring the work. The primary channel is having employees who are more closely engaged in the details of the work take greater ownership of and responsibility for key decisions. They can do so because they are given greater authority and autonomy to make on-the-spot decisions that address issues that come up in the work processes.

The employees often need higher-order thinking and problem-solving skills, which means training incumbent employees to do their jobs differently and/or bringing in new people who can perform at that higher level of complexity and cognitive demand. That often means having to pay them more. However, the net impact on profitability should be neutral to positive, because you need fewer managers (so higher employee costs are offset by lower manager costs) and the team should have greater productivity and quality (so there are lower total unit costs compared to traditional work design).

Even if your leaders aren't explicitly pushing for something like a high performance work design, the diagnostics I describe here and in chapters 6 and 10 regardless are useful to employ. Do your leaders ever exhort the organization to do more with less? To increase productivity even while they try to hold the line on salaries and total labor costs? Sometimes efforts like that work, and often they don't. Strategic Analytics can help identify the reasons why such efforts succeed or fail.

At the team level, the design choice is whether the team is more versus less self-managing. What decisions can the team make on its own versus deferring to others? Would increased team autonomy improve decision making effectiveness and productivity? The benefits of self-managing teams include the ability to solve problems at the point where they occur, leading to quicker resolution, fewer errors, and greater productivity. The tradeoff is that the entire system has to be designed to support self-management. Key elements include hiring and developing different employee skills (greater problem solving, ability to work autonomously, team collaboration, etc.), structuring rewards and performance management to emphasize group collaboration, and so on.

DIFFERENT ORGANIZATIONAL FORMS AND DECISION RIGHTS ALLOCATION

The following discussion of different organizational forms draws heavily from Galbraith's (2014) description of the evolution of organization design as companies grow.

The vast majority of organizations are single business unit, smaller companies. The firm is organized around functions such as sales, marketing, operations, product development, finance, IT, and human resources. Primary decision rights for many strategic issues are concentrated in certain functions, depending on the company's strategy. In many consumer goods companies, sales and marketing have the lion's share of primary decision rights. In many technology companies, product development takes the lead. In electricity generation and utilities, the operations division typically is the most important. And so on. Cross-functional, lateral integration of the work occurs via informal processes, formal teams, and/or matrix reporting relationships. However, because the lateral organization is usually secondary in decision rights to the lead vertical (functional) organization(s), lateral integration is the most common source of breakdown in strategy execution.

As companies grow in size and complexity, the way primary decision rights are assigned evolves away from an exclusive focus on functions. The second stage occurs when the company diversifies into multiple businesses, requiring separate business units with a degree of independent decision making across the business units. Not all decision making is made by the business units, except in cases of pure holding companies. For all other company types, integration across the business units, whether weak or strong, is achieved by reserving some decision rights in the center, with both the senior leadership team and with the functions. In this two-dimensional matrix form, both the business units and functions have primary authority to make some decisions, and the senior leadership team is responsible for making the ultimate decision in cases where conflicts between the business units and functions cannot be resolved by those two groups alone. Lateral integration occurs between and among the business units and functions.

The third stage of evolution occurs when the company expands internationally to the point where some decision rights have to be assigned to each (major) country or region of the globe. When geographies are introduced as decision-making units, the business units and functions maintain some of their historical decision-making authority but at a reduced level.

The fourth stage involves creating units that focus on global customers that are served across the different countries or global regions. This stage also may involve creating units that focus on solutions that cut across global customers. It includes further dividing up of decision rights and heightened complexity of work processes and integration.

When each additional layer of complexity is added to the matrix, some decision rights are assigned to the new operating unit, while other decision rights remain with the traditional operating units, and integration of work processes must occur over more and more dimensions to ensure alignment with the strategy. The implication for analytics is that these larger, more complex organizations have more fronts where measurements of alignment, effective information sharing and collaboration, and strategy execution are needed. Regardless of the number of dimensions of the matrix, though, the analytics focus is the same in all cases: what organizational capabilities are we trying to develop and sustain? How does the organization's design enable (or get in the way of) those capabilities?

KEY ORGANIZATION CAPABILITY QUESTIONS

- What contribution does each role play in creating the organization capability?
- Where is process excellence at odds with the need for local adaptability?
- Are resources properly allocated to support the strategy?
- What are the interdependencies among the roles? How important is group collaboration and performance versus individual job performance?

Organizational Capability Analytics

Organizational capability analytics are the source of many misdiagnoses that lead to poor decision making and failed strategy execution. This occurs in part because organizational capability analytics rarely are conducted comprehensively enough. Senior leaders delegate strategy execution to people who are closer to the work to ensure the tasks get performed correctly. Yet delegation of strategy execution and delegation of analysis are two different things.

Proper analysis of strategy execution has to take place at least partly at an enterprise level. In the Strategic Analytics approach this means starting with step 1 to first identify what the critical organizational issues are that need to be addressed, which organizational capabilities are involved, and whether the focus should be at the enterprise/cross-functional level, or at a sub-group level. Delegation of analysis is appropriate only if the correct focus of the analysis is the sub-group and not enterprise-wide and cross-functional processes. Assessing how effectively lateral integration and cross-functional collaboration take place requires an analytical perspective that transcends functional boundaries.

For example, the IT function has a role to play in strategy execution, and IT needs to take ownership for the tasks that are completely under its control. That is appropriate delegation of strategy execution. If there are general issues about a failure to execute the strategy, however, IT usually does not have the breadth of sight across the entire organization to diagnose the sources of that failure; they can only speak definitively about the tasks under their immediate control.

Even more important is the issue of budget constraints. If there were no budget constraints—if an organization could spend money limitlessly—then there would never be an issue of organizational capability: if the organization lacked some critical capability, it could hire as many people as necessary to solve the problem. The reality of course is the opposite: there are very strong restrictions on spending, and the overwhelming majority of expenditures in organizations are prescribed by the annual budgeting process and divided among many different decision makers.

Where organizational capabilities are strong, most of the mistakes come from assuming either that the capabilities can be strengthened too cheaply or that spending on the capabilities can be reduced without degrading them. For example, in most business units and functions labor costs are typically among the largest expenditures, if not the largest. Because there is not an automatic, one-to-one link between individual competencies and organizational capability, when organizations try to minimize costs, investing a little bit less in paying people today is not going to lead to an immediate degradation in organizational capability. To the contrary, balancing the P&L on the backs of frontline employees can be a very effective way to meet short-term financial targets, at least for a few quarters or even a year or two. But this can lead to a false sense of security that organizational capability will not be degraded while labor costs continue to be cut.

The problem is that managers typically do not stay in a role long enough to be held accountable for the longer-term impacts of their decisions. Cutting labor costs over and over again will eventually degrade organizational capability. If you wait until you clearly see that the capability has diminished, it can be too late to reverse the decline without opening the door for competitors to make inroads into your business. By the time it becomes clear that the cuts were too deep, the managers who made the cuts typically have been promoted. Rather than take responsibility for the negative impact of their cuts, they blame the new managers for the poor performance. In some cases you may have to invest in capabilities simply to maintain performance at current levels.

What contribution does each role play in creating the organization capability? The first step is to map out the contribution that each role makes to creating or enabling the specific organizational capability. For which roles is contributing to the capability a core part of their job responsibility versus a sideline activity? All roles have many different responsibilities and objectives. People whose primary responsibilities are focused on supporting the capability should be expected to do it as part of their jobs; if not, they should be held directly accountable as part of the performance management process. To the extent they don't, the diagnosis should examine whether the problem arises from an individual capability gap, a problem with how their job is designed, and/or their individual motivation (chapter 6).

The situation is more complicated when there are people who make important contributions but the contributions they make represent minor parts of their overall job responsibilities. For example, people in support roles like IT, HR, and finance provide critical inputs for most teams to succeed. However, the support provided to a particular team from any function typically is one of many competing priorities for the support staff assigned to that team. For these types of roles—non-core but still essential contributors—the diagnosis needs to look at a broader set of issues. How are tasks prioritized in the support functions? How do they help address (or not) the needs of a particular team?

More generally, the diagnosis should look at the boundaries between the team's responsibilities and the responsibilities of other teams, functions, and business units. Are the respective responsibilities and accountabilities sufficiently well-defined, or are there unclear boundaries? Where could improvements be made?

Where is process excellence at odds with the need for local adaptability? A full systems diagnosis will look in depth at the conflicts that arise between the needs of a particular team or business process and the enterprise rules created to enforce consistency and discipline across the organization (and prevent reinventing the wheel). People in support functions are responsible for designing and implementing consistent processes across the organization to minimize duplication of effort and maximize efficient use of resources. Because these functions do not have a direct line of sight into the complete set of processes and actions through which organizational capabilities are deployed in the business, their pursuit of function-specific process excellence can work at cross-purposes with maximizing organizational capability. Examples include (a) finance rules requiring proof of ROI for expenditures above a certain amount, (b) inflexible IT systems that cannot respond to locally differentiated needs, and (c) HR processes that focus on uniformity across all employees when differentiation may be required for strategic success.

Conflicts between running consistent enterprise-wide processes and adapting to local needs arise often around core operations as well. National or even global processes for manufacturing, customer engagement, supply chain management, go-to-market distribution systems, sales, marketing, and more can all run into problems when implemented in specific geographies or for particular customer segments that deviate from the norm. When things aren't going well, the tendency is to challenge the local site on why they aren't following the prescribed enterprise processes. A complete Strategic Analytics diagnostic does not automatically assume all fault lies with the local team deviating from standard practice. Rather, the entire situation is examined to determine the extent to which the enterprise-wide processes are the best ones in the specific context, whether problems are created by the local team going against the enterprise-wide processes, or some of both.

For example, customers in a particular market may need bigger price breaks because local competition is much greater than in other markets. Or they may need more time and attention from sales and customer service personnel because they have unusual, nonstandard ways of using the products and services. Or the local infrastructure may be more decrepit and less advanced than that of other geographies, requiring longer delivery times and more customized vehicles than is the norm. And so on.

Are resources properly allocated to support the strategy? Organizations are defined by their strengths, and that's perfectly fine. Many consumer product organizations are marketing driven. Technology companies typically are defined by innovation. High-end consumer retail companies are often fanatical about customer service. In each of these types of organization, it usually is easier to get more resources dedicated toward improving those strengths.

Doubling down on your core strengths sometimes is the right thing to do, but not always. If you can build capabilities that minimize the current weaknesses in your competitive situation and become more ambidextrous (chapter 4), that can be more effective at executing your strategy than focusing only on your strengths. For large consumer products companies, this means getting better at creating breakthrough innovations and integrating them earlier into go-to-market systems. For technology companies that rely on innovation, it could mean learning some lessons on making money through scale and efficiency. For pharmaceutical companies, it could mean learning how to make money on non-branded products to complement the ups and downs of the R&D cycle.

The decision to focus on minimizing weaknesses is a strategic one, but one that cannot be made successfully by senior leaders on their own. The organization's ability to overcome those weaknesses successfully depends on a robust work design that is aligned with the right employee accountabilities, skills, motivation, coordination and support—in other words, is the system designed properly? You can answer that question only through doing integrated enterprise and human capital analytics.

When you are analyzing the performance of a particular group within the organization, a key question about resource allocation is whether leadership provides the support and resources the group needs to succeed. If you want to understand the sources of strategy execution failure, this kind of question is critical to address. You need to know whether the group's problems arise simply from internal problems or because it also had insufficient support from the rest of the organization.

A related resource allocation issue is the compensation paid for the role. Because labor costs make up a large portion (often the majority) of costs for most products and services, there is constant pressure to keep them in check. But the proper amount of compensation to pay is not dictated by what you can get away with. Instead it depends on the job demands—the levels of productivity and quality needed for effective strategy execution. High-performance jobs often require greater compensation to attract and retain people capable of performing at the desired levels (chapter 10).

Are you focusing on areas where making a change would make a difference? Roles often are classified as important or critical based on their average contribution (chapter 10). However, average contribution is not the same as the potential for improvement. This is a key observation by Boudreau and Ramstad in their book *Beyond HR* (2007): the greatest improvements in productivity and effective strategy execution may come from roles that are viewed as not critically important, if importance equals average contribution. The following example from their book helps to illustrate the point.

Consider package delivery and logistics companies and their go-to-market systems, which are described in chapter 9. Two roles in that system are airplane pilots and delivery drivers. The productivity of the airline pilots is greater on average than that of the delivery drivers, and their performance is already highly optimized: room for improvement among the airline pilots is very small. We don't see planes regularly falling from the sky because the organizational systems ensure there is very little variation in productivity. The consequence is that there is little room for improvement in performance of the pilots—they are already performing at the upper range of what is possible.

Greater improvement in organizational capability may be realized by investing in roles that have lower productivity on average, such as the delivery drivers. In contrast with the pilots, there is much greater variability in the performance of the drivers. The work system of the delivery drivers is not as tightly controlled and optimized as that of the pilots because the downside risk of bad delivery performance is relatively minor—it pales in comparison to the catastrophic results that can occur with poor pilot performance. So there could be greater room for improving the work system and performance of the delivery drivers.

The tendency to focus on average contribution instead of opportunities for marginal improvement is endemic in analyses of organizational performance. People everywhere fall for the allure of focusing on the "big" roles—the roles that have truly major impact on organizational performance—because if things go wrong with those roles, then performance can be hurt greatly. These typically include higher-level management roles, sales roles (in marketing-led companies), R&D roles (in innovation-driven companies), and so on. Yet because those roles are so important, they tend to get too much time, attention, and fine tuning, leaving other roles in a state of relative neglect. Optimizing organizational performance so the entire system works at maximum capacity and effectiveness means looking for improvements wherever they should be made. This often means paying more attention to roles that traditionally are neglected.

What are the interdependencies among the roles? How important is group collaboration and performance versus individual job performance? Traditionally neglected roles can be important sources of capability improvement because of interdependencies across roles. "Interdependencies" is just a technical way of saying that no person is an island when it comes to strategy execution and organizational effectiveness: every person and every role relies on other people and roles to get their work done. Another way of stating the point made in the discussion immediately preceding this is that interdependencies raise the importance of traditionally neglected roles.

Airplane pilots' jobs are highly optimized, with advanced computer systems designed to keep their job performance within a narrow band. Delivery truck drivers, in contrast, operate with much greater leeway and ability to do the job differently. If the efficiency of delivery truck drivers can be improved, a greater volume of higher value items can be routed through the system, including on the planes, which raises the productivity of everyone involved in the system, including the pilots (whose planes are flying at fuller capacity). So the pilots' and drivers' jobs are interdependent.

The interdependency that exists between the pilots and drivers is more "loose": the productivity of one group can impact that of the other, but only via the volume and type of packages that flow through the system and the timing of the packages' trip through their part of the distribution system. For most aspects of their respective jobs, though, the jobs are essentially independent. Once a driver's truck is loaded, the pilot has zero impact on the driver's ability to meet route-based objectives of delivery times. Similarly, once the plane is loaded, the driver has zero impact on the pilot's objective of safe and timely flying from one destination to another.

Other roles exhibit much greater interdependency, though. Each pilot has a co-pilot, and those two roles are almost totally interdependent: one person cannot do his or her job without the other also doing the job the right way at the same time. For the delivery driver, there are other roles (like the distribution center workers and maintenance engineers) on which they are more interdependent than the pilots. However, for the most part the delivery driver has independent control over the aspects of the job and does not have to rely on other roles to perform most critical job tasks successfully.

For highly independent roles like the delivery driver, you can focus on job design analytics to understand how well optimized the job is for the tasks at hand and the people who staff it. For interdependent roles like the pilot, you need to do analysis of the group dynamics: do they operate as a well-integrated group or more like a collection of individuals? If they operate more like a group of individuals and do not sufficiently coordinate their work with each other, that lack of coordination usually is a prime source of problems with strategy execution. In that case, the diagnostic needs to examine the team dynamics. See the next section for details on conducting diagnostics of group dynamics.

Once the diagnostics of group effectiveness have been completed, the question for the analysis is whether the roles within the group could be structured differently to improve overall performance. A central objective of the analysis should be to look out for possible redesigns of the work that might increase accountability and motivation for performing the tasks needed to achieve the group's objectives.

KEY CULTURE AND GROUP BEHAVIORS QUESTIONS

- What behaviors does the organization's culture encourage and support? Are they consistent with strategy execution and organizational effectiveness?
- How does the organization design, including rewards, reinforce the culture?
- Do teams operate effectively to accomplish their goals?

Culture and Group Analytics

What behaviors does the organization culture encourage and support? Are they consistent with strategy execution and organizational effectiveness? Organizational culture is correctly acknowledged as a powerful force that drives many behaviors, both positive and negative. When culture helps you accomplish strategic objectives, it's an asset. When it gets in the way, it's a liability. A large part of the power of culture comes from its durability, which also means changing the culture can be a daunting task.

Culture and the organization's design are very closely related. Organizational development experts have long recognized that design and culture are two halves of the same whole. The organization's design is the structure that provides the foundation for the roles that people play and the incentives that guide people to do what they do. The people who populate the roles provide an independent contribution to the culture, which is separate from the design. At the same time, there is a very close link between the design and culture, because the roles and incentives strongly shape people's behaviors: the behaviors are the outward manifestation of the culture.

For example, the culture in pharmaceutical and health care organizations tends to be deliberative and cautious, reflecting organizational strategies that emphasize high quality of drugs and patient care to ensure that deadly mistakes are not made. The culture in consumer products companies tends to emphasize frugality and efficiency, reflecting organizational strategies that emphasize making money off high-volume products sold at small margins. The roles and incentives in both types of organization tend to encourage hiring and retention of personality types that are consistent with the culture. For pharmaceutical and health care companies, this means people who are trained in research, who rely on large amounts of data to make decisions, and who often need to see very strong data-based evidence against an existing policy before deciding to change it. For consumer products companies, in contrast, this means people who are trained in sales and marketing, who rely partly on data and partly on intuition about what drives consumer behaviors.

When the design, people, and behaviors are optimized to reinforce each other, the resulting culture can be incredibly strong and resilient. When there are disconnects or less-than-perfect alignment, the culture is often weaker. Strategic Analytics provides insights into what makes the culture stronger versus weaker by analyzing each component, comparing the reality of how things are with the ideal of how they should be under perfect alignment. The results can be used to determine actions that can either strengthen the existing culture or change it to something entirely different.

How does the organization design, including rewards, reinforce the culture? Understanding the role of performance management and rewards is a central component of culture analytics: those systems are set up to support the primary strategic objectives. A key challenge is that incentives and rewards cannot be all expressed in monetary terms. Compensation is too blunt a tool, so we encourage the behaviors needed for effective strategy execution by evaluating and rewarding them using a variety of "soft" approaches. These include direct feedback, public celebrations of key contributions, access to developmental opportunities, assignment to high-profile tasks and teams, and opportunities for promotion. The combination of hard and soft rewards contributes a great deal to the organizational culture.

Identifying the aspects of performance management and rewards that reinforce the culture is another key task for culture analytics. For example, operating at high levels of scale with great efficiency is a core capability of the go-to-market systems in consumer products, package delivery, and many other industries. The leading companies in those industries often have multiple billion-dollar business lines, which are the foundation of a majority of their financial performance and return to shareholders. Jobs and incentives are carefully designed to promote the success of the billion-dollar business lines.

Yet designing the jobs and incentives that way also creates problems with growing new business lines that could become future billion-dollar brands. When salespeople are rewarded for the total volume of sales, they may shy away from promoting new products that have much more uncertain sales prospects. When operations leaders are rewarded for overall efficiency and cost minimization, they may resist building capabilities that would enable more nimble responses to the market: ones that require greater investment to build new capability without the guarantee of greater sales. Thus comprehensive culture analytics examines not just observed behaviors but also the organizational systems and incentives that promote and reward those behaviors.

Do teams operate effectively to accomplish their goals? Another aspect of culture analytics focuses on diagnosing the factors underlying group dynamics. Culture, more often than not, is the expression of collective behaviors at the group level, not the individual level. Performance is also much more often a group, not individual, phenomenon: only in rare cases do individuals drive business performance singlehandedly (for example certain sales roles, some call-center jobs, and so on). In all other cases, performance is the product of a team or group working together effectively to produce an output for which they are jointly and collectively responsible.

Despite the importance of groups for driving performance and defining organizational culture, many annual employee surveys over-emphasize individually focused questions at the expense of group-focused questions. This reflects a general bias in HR toward focusing on individual-level issues, including developmental plans, performance feedback, compensation that is heavily weighted toward individually controlled factors, and more. Despite the impression created by this overemphasis on individually focused survey items, the analytics of group dynamics are very well developed, including many well-established measures of group dynamics and organizationally-focused factors: team commitment, organization commitment, shared understanding, trust, integration, group-based rewards, and more.

The importance of team diagnostics cannot be overstated. Most HR systems (performance management, career development, competencies, and others) are highly focused on individuals. Even when responsibility for contributing to the group is included as part of the job description and accountabilities, there typically is too little emphasis on team dynamics.

Specific group-oriented questions for Strategic Analytics focus on whether the team members have the responsibility, skills, motivation, coordination, and support needed to accomplish the group's objectives, and they include the following examples. If the team is not accomplishing its objectives, how much is due to a lack of alignment within the team on what they are supposed to accomplish and the methods for doing so (shared understanding)? Are the team's goals set appropriately? Do the team members trust and support each other in getting their work done in the right way at the right time (task-based trust)? Do they proactively share information with each other to eliminate problems before they occur? Are the team members committed to the team (team commitment)? Is the group collectively held accountable for and rewarded for the group's performance? And are the team's actions focused on producing the operational outcomes needed for successful strategy execution? Answering these and related questions can successfully diagnose many sources of strategy execution failure.

The science behind team dynamics diagnostics is quite well developed and documented in the research literature, but less well known within organizations. The good news is there are well-established measures, such as the ones described above and more, that can be used to evaluate team dynamics through interviews or surveys. My book *Employee Surveys That Work* has examples of specific questions that can be used to measure these constructs and more. My colleagues and I at the Center for Effective Organizations, and many of our peers working in research and consulting roles with organizations, have used measures like these for successful group diagnosis for decades.

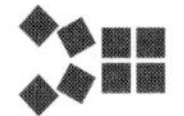

Chapter 6

Step 3—Human Capital Analytics

Issues Addressed in This Chapter

- Step 3 in Strategic Analytics: How to conduct diagnostics at the role, individual, and/or HR process levels
- Job design diagnostics: increasing productivity through job redesign, understanding interdependencies
- Individual capability diagnostics: competency improvement, build versus buy
- Attitude and motivation diagnostics: what factors matter most

Key Questions

- Is the job designed appropriately to justify the performance expectations? Is enough money invested in the role's compensation?

- Could greater productivity be achieved if the job were enriched or enlarged?
- Do the incumbents have the capabilities required by the design?
- What is the cost of developing the competencies from within versus hiring from outside?
- Are people motivated to do the work and perform at the levels required by the design?
- What attracts people to come work for the organization, and what keeps them from leaving?

Chapter 5 covered the three parts of enterprise analytics: organizational capability, organization design, and culture. In this chapter we now turn to the third step in Strategic Analytics, human capital analytics.

HR and frontline managers too often focus human capital analytics on the wrong questions because they improperly prioritize what to analyze. Lower-level HR and frontline managers typically do not have clear lines of sight into which issues should be addressed first, especially when key factors are outside their span of control. The end result is that they perform uncoordinated human capital analytics on a myriad of topics across the organization with no integration back into the strategic priorities and goals. The lack of coordination means that even when HR or frontline managers in one part of the organization come up with insights on top strategic priorities that could have a major impact, they usually lack the ability to get senior leaders to pay attention. The answer is to integrate what they do into the enterprise analytics described in the previous chapter.

Just like enterprise analytics, human capital analytics also has three parts: individual capability, job design, and attitudes/motivation. Each of the three components of human capital analytics is often applied in isolation. Strategic Analytics addresses all three for deeper insights into the motivation and performance drivers for a role.

The three parts of human capital analytics are represented by the three parts of human capital performance in the top part in the causal model in figure 5 (chapter 1) and are repeated here in figure 10.

Just as with the previous chapter, the best way to use this chapter is to read the entire thing first. Each section raises specific questions that you should be able to answer when doing a complete Strategic Analytics diagnostic. The key questions posed at the beginning of each section can be used as a launching point for designing an interview protocol for conducting stakeholder interviews. The details within each section provide guidance for how to probe deeper on any issue that emerges

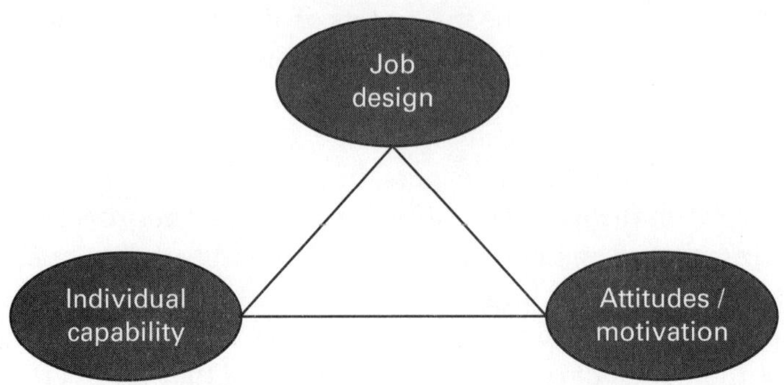

Figure 10: Human Capital Analytics Components

as a more likely cause where you need additional details for a complete diagnostic. The appendix provides an interview template that incorporates the human capital diagnostic questions from this chapter and the enterprise diagnostic questions from chapter 5.

Job design analysis focuses on the individual job role and its responsibilities, and the potential for improving performance through altering the job design. These issues often are not considered for individual jobs outside of a larger organization or business unit redesign. Yet that is all the more reason why Strategic Analytics includes job design analytics. You need to understand the structural issues to properly diagnose challenges with motivation and behavior.

Individual capability analysis addresses the competencies needed for the role, how long it takes to achieve full productivity in the role, and the build versus buy decision for developing and retaining the capability. A key issue is whether the expectations for performance are consistent with the talent available to staff the role, both internally and externally.

Individual-level attitudes analytics focus on motivation and engagement. Why do people choose to do what they do? How are they influenced and impacted by the organization and the people with whom they work?

KEY JOB DESIGN QUESTIONS

- Is the job designed appropriately given the expectations for performance?
- Could greater productivity be achieved if the job were enriched or enlarged?
- How interdependent is the job on other roles in the organization?

Job Design Analytics

It is hard to design jobs to deliver the performance required by the strategy. One of the biggest problems is the challenge of achieving high performance in a particular role when capabilities and motivation vary across individuals. Annual budgeting decisions over the amount of money to spend on a role depend on what levels of performance one can expect to achieve from the average person in the role. The challenge for job design is finding the right match between the job requirements and the available pool of people.

No job can be perfectly designed on paper. The design has to be tested in practice, with the different parts examined for how well they fit together. Do the people have the capabilities required by the design? Are they motivated to do the work and perform at the levels required by the design?[2]

Annual budgeting decisions put strict limits on how much compensation can be paid for a role. The budgeting decisions assume that the compensation is sufficient to attract and retain

[2]These three components together define the Capability-Opportunity-Motivation (COM) model that social scientists have long used to examine the drivers of performance in a role (Blumberg and Pringle, 1982). From the perspective of the individuals in the role, the design creates (or inhibits) the "opportunity" to perform. I use the term "design" here instead of "opportunity" because it reflects the choice organizations have when deciding what a role should be.

people with the right skills who also will be motivated to deliver the desired performance. If problems with productivity arise, diagnosis attempts almost always focus on either the capability of the people in the role or their motivation. The fundamental job design rarely is raised as a factor because that would mean challenging the assumptions made by the annual budgeting process. Such a challenge might seem like a threat to senior leaders who do the budgeting, so lower-level managers and analysts almost always leave design questions unaddressed and focus only on the other two components. That leaves a gap for Strategic Analytics to address.

Some very important job design factors have to be included in the inquiry if you want to get to the root of what drives performance in a role. Two important ones are (a) job enrichment and enlargement, and (b) interdependencies and joint accountabilities between roles.

Job enrichment and enlargement. Getting greater productivity and engagement from workers through job enrichment is an idea that has been around for decades. It is just as relevant today as when Richard Hackman and Edward Lawler first introduced it in 1971. An enriched job has greater skill variety, autonomy, and feedback, among other characteristics. An enlarged job, in contrast, is one that has more of the same tasks without changing the variety of tasks. A key question to ask when doing human capital analytics is the potential for productivity improvement under enriched or enlarged jobs.

Organizations constantly attempt to increase productivity by redesigning processes so that greater output can be achieved with minimal increases in headcount. When jobs are enriched, workers' intrinsic motivation to perform the tasks can increase, which supports increased productivity. If the jobs become less enriched, this can make the work less interesting and intrinsically motivating to perform.

Job enlargement can also increase productivity because more tasks are performed by the same worker. If the initial workload is reasonable for the time allotted and the compensation paid, adding additional work may increase productivity with no negative consequences. However, increasing the workload too much can lead to stress and burnout from work-life imbalance.

The level of compensation for a role can play an important part in both cases. Would the incumbent employees be able to perform an enriched job successfully with additional training and experience, or would they have to be replaced by people better suited to do the new work? Enriched jobs often require higher-level skills, so compensation often needs to be higher to attract and retain the people capable of performing at the higher level of productivity. Enlarged jobs do not necessarily require greater skills, but they can be more strenuous than other jobs the person could find elsewhere. Would the incumbents be overwhelmed with the work load if the job were enlarged, would they find the greater variety of tasks more interesting, or perhaps both? Depending on how the jobs are changed and how the incumbents perceived the changes, compensation may or may not have to change with job enlargement.

When conducting Strategic Analytics, you cannot take the role as given and assume no changes can be made. In order to provide the deepest insights into how to improve strategy execution and investment in the strategy, the analysis must consider scenarios in which jobs are redesigned to make them more or less enriched, and more or less enlarged. This includes testing annual budget allocation assumptions about attracting and retaining the right types of employees to work in the role. Whether senior leaders take actions on the analysis results is a separate matter; the analysis itself is critical. A more in-depth discussion of analyzing compensation and high performance work design is provided in chapter 10.

Interdependencies and joint accountabilities. Very few critical tasks in organizations are performed solely by one role. Most key tasks require input and coordination from multiple roles, which creates interdependency among the roles. For example, delivering a good customer service experience requires more than what salespeople or call center representatives can do on their own: input and coordination from other roles that support customer service processes, such as IT and operations, are central as well. Go-to-market systems, R&D, manufacturing, supply chain, and virtually all other processes in organizations occur only because people in many different roles work together interdependently. Chapter 1 provides examples of the exceptions to the rule about interdependencies: certain jobs exist in sales and customer service where the contribution to strategy execution can be largely independent of other roles in the organization.

The problem is how to hold people in interdependent roles accountable for their contribution to the group's performance. Performance management systems are built to help ensure that people will perform the right behaviors and that they will be held accountable for their actions. If the outcome the organization desires doesn't occur, how can individuals be held accountable? The interdependency typically makes it difficult or even impossible for an outside observer to discern completely who performed which actions and who might have fallen short of doing everything they were supposed to do. Accountability may be possible only at the team level.

A related problem is that each role in an organization typically is responsible for a large number of tasks and objectives. The people performing that role have to prioritize which tasks are most important to ensure that nothing critical is neglected. How they prioritize often depends on their views of what is important, combined with a personal preference for doing some tasks over others. In the end, some strategically important tasks may not be performed properly.

Job design analytics has to examine the actions expected from the role, the likely reasons those actions were not performed perfectly, and potential solutions to improve performance and accountability. The potential solutions include both formal systems, like performance management and rewards, as well as "softer" ways of getting people to behave through influence and appealing to their sense of organizational citizenship, commitment to their teammates, and other factors. Chapter 10 presents additional details on understanding the role of the individual versus the group in contributing to organizational effectiveness, including analyzing the design features of performance management, rewards, and accountability that support strategy execution.

KEY INDIVIDUAL CAPABILITY QUESTIONS

- Do the incumbents have the capabilities required by the design?
- Build versus buy: What is the cost of developing the competencies from within versus hiring from outside?
- Which competencies can be more readily learned through training and which through on-the-job experience?

Individual Capability Analytics

Three main issues are addressed by capability analytics: (1) what are the competencies needed for performance and how should they be prioritized, (2) how can the competency gap among current employees be closed, and (3) whether compensation is sufficient to attract and retain people who can perform at the expected productivity level.

Identifying and prioritizing tasks and competencies. The first task for capability analytics is to identify and prioritize which tasks and competencies are most relevant for the issue being investigated. A simple list of competencies or tasks that are central for strategy execution contains no information about when and how the competencies should be applied or the tasks executed. This lack of information is a key issue I see over and over again when doing work with companies. It usually is easy to say "we have a problem" and point to the part of organization and processes where the problem arises. The real challenge is figuring out if people are doing the right tasks in the right ways at the right time. That is where the true measurement challenge exists.

A related issue is differentiating role tasks versus individual competencies. Competencies are defined as the ability to demonstrate a behavior, not the extent to which people apply the behavior in specific contexts. People can be highly rated on a set of competencies and still fall short in applying them in one or more settings: their high rating comes from what they do in general and usually not from what they do once throughout the entire year. However, if that one instance is critical for strategy success, a single failure then means a failure in strategy execution. The individual's peers and supervisor might dismiss the single instance, ascribing it to bad luck or having a bad day, and not reduce their rating of the person's competency. Nonetheless, it led to a failure to execute the strategy. Looking at competency data alone cannot trace the cause: only through in-depth interviews and/or observations can we diagnose the issues the right way.

Build versus buy for closing the competency gap. It is almost always cheaper to build capability by developing people from within than by hiring them from outside, if current employees can be successfully developed in a short enough time frame. The closing of their competency gaps happens through a combination of on-the-job experience and training.

The job for analytics in this case is to investigate the efficacy of both experience and training in closing the competency gaps. Are some competencies more easily learned through one approach or the other? Are there some gaps that cannot be closed easily? How much time and investment does it take to close the gaps with internal candidates, and how does that compare to paying open market prices and hiring from outside? Is there a ready supply of external hires that can be brought in to make up the difference? Is compensation for the role sufficient to attract and retain the people who can perform at the expected productivity level? Do the economics of hiring from outside make a stronger argument for developing from within, even if that means dealing with the competency gaps for a longer period of time?

Chapter 12 addresses these questions in greater detail, including analyzing the potential benefits of redesign as a third option.

Attracting and retaining the right talent. One of the most important roles compensation plays is attraction and retention. How do the job demands compare to those of alternative jobs in the local labor market? What has happened to external benchmarks of compensation: has compensation risen to keep pace with inflation, has it exceeded inflation, or has it stagnated? With those objectives in mind, compensation for each role is calibrated against comparable alternative jobs in the local labor market. The question is how to set the compensation relative to the benchmark.

Typically two competing views on this question come from different voices in the organization. Finance and many general managers usually try to keep compensation as low as possible and focus on setting compensation close to the median benchmark, if not lower. As one general manager expressed to me, "Why should we pay more to everyone in the job just to try and attract a few better people? Raising compensation for everyone in the job rewards all the people including the average performers." This view assumes that a typical (average) candidate hired from outside represents the kind of person the organization needs, in terms of both ability and desire to perform at that compensation level.

The counterview often comes from the direct supervisors and their leaders, who are held accountable for the group's performance and who are not responsible for the labor budget. They are happy to spend more on higher-quality people who can easily get the work done. They often argue that the job demands are more stringent than those of alternative jobs in the local labor market. If they are correct, then the average person hired from outside will have a lower probability of being productive in the role. If the productivity demands of the job have increased over time but those of alternative external jobs have not have changed as much, their fear of losing people may be quite legitimate.

The only way to reconcile these two views on setting and calibrating compensation is through analytics. How do the job demands compare to those of alternative jobs in the local labor market? What has happened to the benchmark level of external compensation: has it risen to keep pace with inflation or has it stagnated?

The analysis needs to address two complementary questions: If we tried staffing a role with slightly cheaper talent, could the current level of organizational capability be maintained? If we increased the amount of compensation paid to a role, would we be able to attract and retain higher quality talent? See Chapter 10 for further discussion on how to value the contribution of a role in terms of its contribution and the part it plays in supporting high performance.

KEY INDIVIDUAL ATTITUDES AND MOTIVATION QUESTIONS

- Are people motivated to do the work and perform at the levels required by the design?
- What parts of the job and organization attract them to work for us?
- What keeps them from leaving?
- What makes them committed and willing to go the extra mile?

Individual Attitudes and Motivation Analytics

The motivation to perform is one of the most important factors impacting strategy execution. Even if the design is right and the people are capable of doing the work, a lack of motivation will yield poor performance. Attitudes analytics provide the insights necessary to diagnose many parts of both the employee experience, which impacts motivation, as well as the work design.

The variety of measurements for conducting attitudes analytics often dwarfs that available for the other two types of analytics—design and capability—combined. This is the case because industrial-organizational psychologists have spent decades exploring the various ways that people interact with the job tasks, their colleagues and the environment at work. A comprehensive review of the advances that have been made over the years would require many volumes. The abbreviated discussion here provides a cursory review of the types of measurements that have proven particularly robust at explaining motivation, behavior, and performance for a myriad of job types in a wide variety of work settings. Details on collecting these types of measurements from surveys, along with examples of specific questions to ask, are covered in my book *Employee Surveys That Work* (Levenson, 2014a).

RANDOM CORRELATIONS OR PARTIAL MODEL TESTING?

Chapter 2 highlighted the dangers of data mining in the discussions of linkage analysis and employee engagement. If you compare any two attitudinal items from a survey, you likely will find a statistically significant relationship. This occurs because of what psychologists call general affect: people who are unhappy are more likely to respond negatively across the board to all survey items that measure how they feel, and vice versa. If you randomly correlate two survey items, you may find some interesting but misleading patterns.

For example, answers to "we have a good process for mentoring employees" might correlate negatively with those to "it is likely that I will quit my job in the next twelve months." But that doesn't mean that improved mentoring would necessarily reduce turnover. Mentoring is only one of many factors that can impact turnover. If there is a strong correlation between mentoring and intention to leave, you can be pretty sure there are similar correlations with many other survey questions. So you need to be careful about jumping to conclusions based on simple comparisons.

On the other side, are all exploratory analyses inappropriate? No, that's also incorrect. Testing a robust causal model often starts with looking at the bivariate relationships between the outcome of interest you care about—turnover, productivity, etc.—and each of the factors that you think drives the outcome. If someone inquires about how two measures are related, like mentoring and intention to leave, it's o.k. to focus on them. Just make sure the analysis is the start of the inquiry. You need to assess a full causal model to know for sure what's really driving behavior or motivation.[3]

Retention models. Retention is a very common concern. One popular method for measuring the factors impacting retention—the exit survey—is generally unreliable. Asking questions such as "why did you leave" typically does not yield the most reliable information. First, people who are leaving often give biased responses because they want to save face or give disproportionate blame to someone or something based on hurt feelings. Second, people who leave are often different from the people who have not left. You cannot project one group's feelings onto the other group.

A better approach to dealing with retention issues is to ask current employees about their intention to leave. Measuring intention to leave is very reliable for predicting turnover. A second major benefit is that all incumbent employees can be asked the questions, which enables a complete profile of the risk of any person in the organization leaving. By matching that

[3]When you estimate a large, multivariate model, it is good practice to make sure first that each of the factors that are included as possible drivers is significantly correlated with the outcome. For example, suppose you hypothesize that developmental opportunities, pay, relationship with supervisor, and support from team members are drivers of intention to leave. Before estimating a multivariate model, first make sure that each factor has a statistically significant relationship to intention to leave. If not, they should be excluded from the larger model. If you are not the person running the analysis, you should review the results from the initial bivariate correlations to make sure everything looks reasonable before looking at results from the multivariate model.

outcome measure (intention to leave) with other questions that measure the drivers of turnover, multivariate statistics can test which factors are most important.

For example, consider the PwC case study from chapter 7 discussed by Levenson, Fenlon, and Benson (2010). PwC wanted to understand the drivers of turnover for a key employee group, and they used intention to leave to measure turnover risk. They identified leading potential causes of turnover and measured those as well: pay satisfaction, anticipated compensation growth at PwC, anticipated compensation growth if the person went somewhere else, perceived availability of alternative jobs, job satisfaction, work-life balance, fit with the industry, whether their skills were being used, and support for professional development. Through multivariate statistical analysis they identified that work-life balance was a much more important driver of turnover than PwC had suspected, leading to a redesign of the changes they had intended to reduce turnover. Those changes were successful.

Examples like this highlight the importance of using multivariate statistics to discover and test the true drivers of employee attitudes. This runs counter to common practice in most organizations, where survey questions are often examined one or two at a time to try to divine relevant insights. As discussed in further detail in *Employee Surveys That Work*, though, there really is no substitute for multivariate analysis in most situations if you want to identify the most important factors driving attitudes.

Understanding the most important drivers of employee attitudes is the one part of Strategic Analytics where advanced statistical analysis is commonly needed. For all the other six parts (competitive advantage, organization design, organization capability, culture and group behaviors, job design, and individual capability), a combination of key stakeholder interviews plus simple data analysis (calculating averages, ranges, differences, etc.) is all that is needed.

Discretionary effort, commitment and thriving/burnout models. Another priority for organizations is discretionary effort.

We want people to dedicate themselves to the work as fully and completely as possible. When it comes to measuring attitudes consistent with discretionary effort, employee attitudes analysis can contribute in some ways and come up short in other ways.

Let's start with the bad news. Many consultants and researchers have discretionary effort measures they claim are actionable. However, consider the likely responses to a question like "I go above and beyond my job duties to do extra for this company." First, people who are more humble are likely to rate themselves lower than people who are more egotistic. However, it is more likely that the more humble people are actually more dedicated and contributing greater discretionary effort than the egotists. Self-reported questions like these can be inaccurate when employees have different self-images.

Second, even if people responded accurately, these measures say nothing about where the effort is applied. Employees who volunteer extra time to help out with social functions at work would say they expend discretionary effort. Yet those kinds of activities rarely contribute to strategic success. Other avenues for discretionary effort are more likely to be important for enhancing strategy execution.

The good news is that there are actionable alternative attitudinal measures that provide meaningful insights. Organizational commitment is a reliable measure of how identified people feel with the company, and it can predict retention (Cohen, 1993). People who are committed to the organization almost certainly are more willing to put in discretionary effort. Measures of thriving or energy at work can be good indicators of how engaging the work is (Porath, Spreitzer, Gibson, and Stevens, 2012). At the other end of the spectrum, burnout can measure whether you are pushing your people too hard, so that you may lose them forever (Cropanzano, Rupp, and Byrne, 2003).

Not all relevant attitudinal and performance measures can be obtained from surveys. In addition to discretionary effort, another prominent example is goal setting. Setting goals that are achievable but somewhat aggressive ("stretch goals") is important for high performance (Latham, 2007). However, self-reported stretch goal questions do not yield reliable data: people have too strong an incentive to exaggerate the difficulty of their goals. Reliable goal setting measures have be collected from people outside the role who can objectively evaluate goal difficulty.

Other critical factors to consider when building and testing models of employee attitudes include the relationship with the employee's supervisor, opportunities for professional development, career satisfaction, and more. Their importance will vary, depending on the roles being examined, the size of the organization and breadth of jobs available internally, individual differences in what the employees want from work, and much more.

It can be easy to feel like you are drowning when you consider the wide range of available employee attitudes measures. Strategic Analytics can help you to stay focused on what you are trying to explain and why. To identify strategy execution drivers, build and test causal models and pay attention to whether individual versus group performance matters. Case study examples follow in the next chapter.

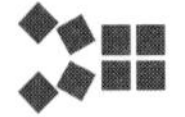

Chapter 7

Putting It All Together

Issues Addressed in This Chapter

- What a complete systems diagnostic looks like
- How to choose between mostly enterprise analysis, mostly human capital analysis, or both
- Case study examples including causal models

Key Questions

- When is it appropriate to focus only on enterprise analysis?
- When is it appropriate to focus primarily on human capital analysis?
- What type of due diligence is needed in each case?

This chapter shows how to pull together the different parts of Strategic Analytics for a complete analysis. The previous three chapters described the details of the different parts. Doing every single element from those chapters is a lot. However, you will *never* have to worry about answering every single question posed in those chapters. Often you can take short cuts, depending on how much time, energy, and resources you have to invest in doing the analytics.

The appendix presents a diagnostic protocol template that you can use for designing the diagnostic you want to perform. It is *not* a predefined tool that requires you to apply every single piece of it. Rather, it is more like a buffet, where the goal is to construct a balanced meal. In order for the diagnostic to be properly balanced, you have to make sure you can address each of the seven parts of Strategic Analytics:

1. Strategic context and causal model
2. Organizational design
3. Organizational capability
4. Culture and group behaviors
5. Job design
6. Individual capability
7. Attitudes and motivation

The appendix lists both the main things you need to know and sample questions to address for each of the categories. No matter what you do, pay attention to the things you need to know for each category. If you are short on time and need to figure out where you can economize, see if you can address those things on your own or with some help from a small number of people in your organization. That can free up time that is best spent on the highest priority categories.

For example, the answers to the questions around the strategic context are usually straightforward to address. Interviews with at most a handful of senior executives should be sufficient to identify the organizational capabilities that support competitive advantage, as well as the changes needed to improve execution of the strategy. Those interviews should also address most of the issues around leaders' willingness to change the organization to reach those objectives. In contrast, constructing the causal model usually requires more time and interviews.

For the other six categories, how much time and effort is needed for each one depends on the particular issue being examined. The examples in this chapter show what a complete diagnostic looks like. In some cases, only a few of the six categories need a lot of time and attention; in other cases it's more of them. Whatever the particulars are in any case, at minimum you have to make sure you know what's going on in each part. If you can be sure of what the issues are in one part, you don't necessarily need to do lots of analysis on it. But you have to do enough to ensure you can explain the complete picture. That's the only way of ensuring you are focusing on the right parts with the right amount of time and effort.

For example, how do you know if it's OK to spend less time on the larger picture of organizational design and focus more narrowly on one job? You must first establish what the strategic objectives are, how they are measured, and the job's role in helping attain those objectives. If you can establish that there are no big issues at the enterprise level, you can focus exclusively on the human capital level; the PwC case discussed later in this chapter is one such example. In order for that more narrow focus to work, once you've done the analysis at the human capital level, go back and double-check that the derived solution will drive the changes needed to achieve the strategic objectives. If not, then you have to take a step back and look at the larger system in which the job is embedded. What else has to take place that is beyond the job's control for improved strategy execution?

In general, the bigger question is how do we know we reached the right conclusions? When is it OK to focus less intensively on either enterprise or human capital analytics? Problems usually arise when a business leader decides to cut the inquiry short on the human capital side, or an HR leader decides to cut it short on the enterprise side. Those biases often create problems because that's their natural tendency—to ignore what they don't know really well.

To avoid those natural biases, both sides need to actively engage someone or some group of people from the other side. It is OK for a business person to deemphasize the human capital side of the analysis only if one or more HR professionals (with really good insights) agree that the human capital issues have been sufficiently addressed. Think about having to present your case to a jury of your peers from the other side. If the business person can convince the HR jury that all relevant issues exist only at the enterprise level, then the bulk or all of the analysis can be focused at the enterprise level. An example of this is provided later in this chapter around the speed of decision making.

On the other side, it is OK for an HR person to deemphasize the enterprise side of the analysis only if a jury of peers from the business side would agree to it. This means making a clear link between the human capital or HR issue and its strategic or bottom-line impact, like in the PwC case.

If neither of those arguments would win the day with either jury, then you need a more balanced approach that looks at both enterprise and human capital issues. That doesn't mean equal time and effort spent on both; rather, some depth of analysis is needed for both sides. An example of this is the Frito-Lay case discussed in this chapter.

Analyses Primarily at the Enterprise Level

Analyses can be conducted primarily at the enterprise level if it can be established definitively that that's the main source of issues with strategy execution. Consider the following two case studies on speed of decision making and an organization's operating model.

Case study 1: Speed of decision making. In this case a company identified a problem with speed of decision making. It held too many meetings that would go on without clear resolution, and important decisions were deferred or delayed.

When the diagnostic was first launched, the issue was framed as inefficient decision making. To identify the appropriate focus, the company followed the Strategic Analytics steps.

Step 1: Identify the sources of competitive advantage and where the problems are. The company produced products for consumers in the pharmaceutical, biotech, and/or medical devices field. Its strategy was to create innovative products that could command high prices while under patent protection. Its competitive advantage came from inventing safe products that generated large sales volumes.

The organizational design split decision-making authority between product development groups responsible for shepherding new ideas through the development process and functions responsible for ensuring best practices in their domains (R&D, quality, manufacturing, sales, and others). The company had a culture that emphasized consensus-based, participative decision making; anyone with a relevant perspective was encouraged to weigh in. Consensus-based decision making also supported the safety objectives: anyone who saw a potential consumer safety issue could raise their hand and object.

The problem was that some important decisions were subject to endless meetings and not resolved in a timely fashion. This threatened the company's ability to capitalize on market opportunities.

Step 2: Enterprise analytics. The enterprise diagnostic looked first at the allocation of decision rights and the culture to identify the potential causes of slow decision making. If the need for analysis at the human capital level emerged as an issue, that would be addressed next. But first the issues at the enterprise level had to be sorted out.

The stakeholder interviews revealed that process-based solutions had been tried in the past, such as rules for decision making in meetings. The rules improved the effectiveness of meetings. However, they did not resolve the issue of who had ultimate decision-making authority. The analysis identified consensus decision making as the main problem.

When the company was much smaller, the consensus culture was not very efficient, but it also wasn't a problem. Most key decision makers were colocated at the company's headquarters so they could gather in one place relatively easily. This brought a wide variety of voices into most decision making, including voices that weren't central to the decisions. This created an inclusive culture, but it also perpetuated the idea that anyone of importance could insert themselves into any discussion.

As the company grew in size, complexity, and geographic reach, the consensus culture became a burden. Functions responsible for product development, quality, and manufacturing all were acutely aware of the need for safety and ensured proper treatment of safety issues. Consensus decision making no longer contributed to improving product safety decisions and thus was not relevant for executing the strategy. To the contrary, the culture enabled people who should not have been involved in key decisions to interject inappropriately, slowing everything down. With more and more key stakeholders operating in different locations, the consensus-driven process was no longer feasible either—it had become an artifact reducing the company's effectiveness.

The enterprise analysis conclusion was that the vast majority of problems with the speed of decision making stemmed from unclear decision rights. The solution required clarifying those decision rights to reduce or remove consensus decision making.

Step 3: Human capital analytics. In this case, no effective argument could be made for conducting human capital analytics at the role or individual levels.

On the job design side, no specific roles emerged as central to increasing the speed of decision making. Were there changes that could be made in the roles and responsibilities for specific jobs that could have increased decision making efficiency and effectiveness? Yes, but the analysis identified a *systemic* issue of decision rights. No one job or a handful of jobs caused the problem. It was a much more diffuse issue of allocation of decision rights among the product groups and functions across the entire company.

In the area of individual capability and motivation, the question previously had been raised regarding people's ability to make decisions more effectively. The specific focus was decision making within meetings. Tools and training on effective decision making were provided but to little effect: the problems with decision making persisted.

Note that the conclusions reached about the relevant elements at the human capital level came about through the stakeholder interviews that covered the enterprise issues. The primary focus of the interviews was the enterprise analysis, but the interviewers also probed for issues rooted in specific roles, individual capability or motivation. The interviewees consistently pointed to larger systemic issues that transcended specific roles, as well as the previous attempts to take process-based approaches to improve decision-making speed (for example, RACI charts). The clear conclusion was that the vast majority of problems existed at the enterprise level, so no further data collection and analysis were needed at the human capital level.

The causal model that emerged from the analysis is shown in figure 11.

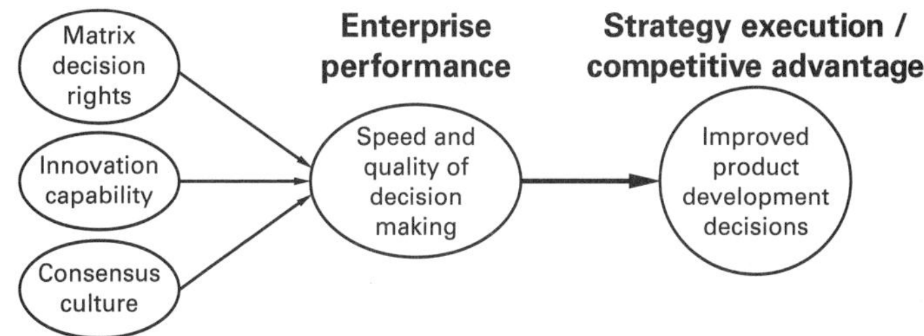

Figure 11: Causal Model for Speed of Decision Making Case Study

Case study 2: Role redundancy. In this case, a company wanted to understand why there was a problem with duplication of roles in the business units and central support functions.

Step 1: Identify the sources of competitive advantage and where the problems are. The company operated manufacturing facilities in many different locations that used heavy machinery. The company's competitive advantage derived from facility locations, access to and price of inputs, and operations excellence. The facilities in different business units (BUs) were in related businesses, so there was some scope for sharing of operations best practices.

The company's legacy was strongly independent BUs. Many historically had their own locally staffed support functions and were used to the speed and responsiveness of that organizational design. On the flip side, that legacy made it hard for the central functions to coordinate their work across the entire organization.

Step 2: Enterprise analytics. The enterprise diagnostic interviews looked specifically at the matrix design and the role of the central support functions. It identified conflict between the BUs and support functions as a key driver of role duplication. The BUs held onto roles that should have been allocated to the functions.

One reason for the role duplication was the culture of BU independence. The BUs were responsible for their own profits and losses (P&L). Many BU leaders preferred having functional roles that reported to them locally. So even though the central functions were supposed to lead the work in their technical domains (finance, IT, HR, and others), the BUs would often lead parallel efforts that were narrowly focused on their individual issues. This led to duplicated efforts and roles and minimized sharing of best practices across the BUs.

The diagnostic determined that the solution to role duplication was clarified function versus BU decision rights and improved functional support. The BUs were instructed to release roles to functional control in exchange for guarantees of improved functional support.

Step 3: Human capital analytics. The human capital diagnostic was not needed in this case because the identified issues originated from conflict between BUs and functions. Of course there were many examples of duplication of tasks within particular roles. But what mattered was the source of duplication. Since it came primarily from the organizational design, unclear decision rights, and a cultural legacy of independent BUs, those issues had to be addressed first.

Though there was no immediate need for a deep human capital diagnostic, the potential for future analysis was identified. Specifically, once the issues were initially resolved at the enterprise level, everyone expected that the duplicated roles and tasks would disappear. What could not be predetermined was the success of those efforts.

There was a distinct possibility that a BU might persist doing things the old way. If that occurred, then there would be justification for a human capital diagnostic. That analysis would focus on the roles and organizational processes that had not adapted to the changes in organizational design. Specific issues to be addressed in the diagnostic would include people's motivation for persisting with the old way of doing things, the rewards and/or consequences they received for doing so, the support they had for moving to the new way of work, and their ability to work the new way. Everyone agreed that any such diagnostic would wait for six months to a year to give people time to adopt the new way of working. That time was needed to determine if the changes had taken root systemically.

Analyses Primarily at the Human Capital Level

Analyses can be conducted primarily at the human capital level if that's the main source of strategy execution issues. Consider the following two case studies. In both only a cursory review of the enterprise issues was needed to determine that the vast majority of the time and effort should be spent on human capital analytics.

Case study 3: Retention of critical talent. PwC (formerly PricewaterhouseCoopers) is an accounting, tax, and consulting services firm with a partnership structure. In 2004 they faced a talent retention issue: too many of their early-career staff were leaving. They wanted to know how to address the issue so that their ability to deliver service to their clients did not suffer. The case study presented here is drawn from Levenson, Fenlon, and Benson (2010) and Levenson (2011); see those sources for further details.

Step 1: Identify the sources of competitive advantage and where the problems are. The client service staff with too much turnover were the firm's senior associates. The firm's partnership structure required a minimum number of people at each level in the career track leading up to partner. If too many people left at one level, there would be too few people available to do the work at higher levels (manager, senior manager, partner). That was the risk the firm needed to minimize.

The importance of the senior associates for competitive advantage was clear and indisputable. PwC provided value to its clients through high-quality tax, accounting, and consulting services. Too few people at any level of the partnership might undermine the delivery of high-quality services.

Step 2: Enterprise analytics. The initial stakeholder interviews established that there was not much to be done in the way of enterprise analytics. The threat to the firm was turnover within a specific role. The business challenge was identified as existing specifically within that role. There was no mandate to focus on large-scale changes to the organizational design or culture—neither one had fundamental problems to be addressed. So the analytics focused exclusively on the human capital level.

Step 3: Human capital analytics. The human capital analytics focused specifically on the factors that were more likely to drive turnover. Interviews of people in the role and their supervisors identified a number of potential factors. The employees' views on those factors were measured using a survey designed specifically for the analysis. A multivariate regression model tested the importance of the factors. The results are summarized in figure 12 in the causal model for this case study.

As expected, the job design analytics identified fit as a potential issue: people who did not prefer these types of jobs in professional service were more likely to leave. However, the firm already had a rigorous process for identifying and screening job candidates, so there was not much room for improvements in this area that might reduce turnover.

Three other factors emerged from the analysis that could be addressed: compensation, career development opportunities, and work-life balance.

Before this analysis, the firm had suspected that compensation was important—so much so that a potential deferred compensation solution had been suggested before the analysis was conducted. The analysis confirmed that compensation was very important for retention. However, it also showed that the

5 to 7 percent raises that client service staff received annually already were strong retention drivers. Any reasonably sized deferred compensation solution (such as a 10 percent bonus for staying five years) would have been small in comparison and not made much of a difference in future retention.

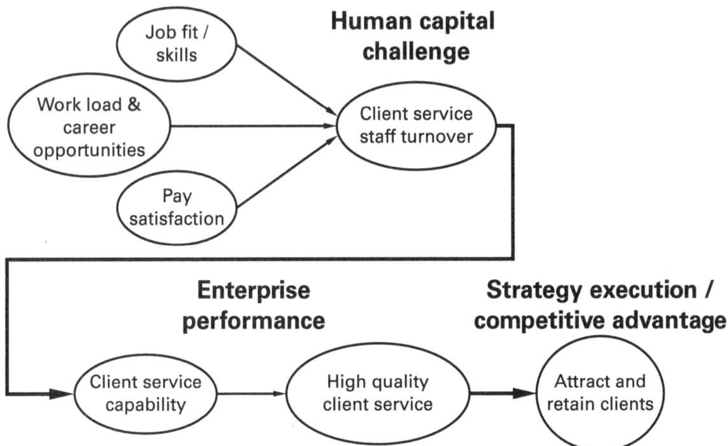

Figure 12: Causal Model for Retention of Critical Talent Case Study

Career development opportunities also emerged as an important area that the firm could address to improve retention. In response the firm worked to increase connectivity between the partners and staff to ensure good lines of communication and appropriate career expectations. They also increased the quality of coaching and development to improve the staff's career experiences.

Work-life balance was a third factor, one that the firm knew could be an issue. The time of year when annual taxes are prepared for submission is extremely busy in the accounting profession. It is common for everyone to work very long hours for three months straight, producing strain and work-life balance problems. So it was not a surprise to hear about work-life balance issues. The important insight from the analysis was that compensation was not the solution (see discussion above) and that work-life balance was a very important factor.

With those answers in hand, the firm did what it could to address work load issues. Tools were developed for team leaders to better manage the work load across team members. Options for more flexible work arrangement were introduced. Where possible, work was "pulled forward" into the month before the busy tax preparation season, lessening the volume of tasks to be done at the busiest time.

Case study 4: Evaluating the impact of executive coaching. Executive coaching is widely used as a tool to improve leadership effectiveness, even though there is little evidence for coaching's impact on organizational performance and strategy execution. Two companies, one in financial services and the other in pharmaceuticals/biotech/medical devices, used Strategic Analytics to evaluate the business impact from executive coaching so that they could improve it. Levenson (2009) has additional details beyond the highlights provided here.

The analysis used interviews with matched coach and coachee pairs to determine whether coaching had a positive impact on strategy execution or financial metrics.

Step 1: Identify the sources of competitive advantage and where the problems are. Executive coaching takes place across a wide variety of industries and strategies, so it's impossible to define a specific competitive advantage. The general problem is finding a link between the leadership behaviors that coaching focuses on and any kind of bottom-line impact.

Step 2: Enterprise analytics. Executive coaching focuses exclusively on the individual leaders, not the systems in which they work. The focus purposefully ignores larger structural issues, even though they may be a major contributing factor to leaders' success. In each individual case, the coach and coachee take structural issues into account to maximize leadership effectiveness. However, there is not much to do to address structural issues when evaluating the impact of coaching. The unique structural issues of each leader's business unit and function cannot be summarized through simple measurements.

Note that the organizational design and culture nonetheless are critically important in defining and constraining leaders' effectiveness. The challenge is that the analysis has to focus exclusively at the human capital level. Once the analysis at the human capital level is completed, the insights can then be interpreted within the organizational context.

Step 3: Human capital analytics. The job design of executives' roles is relevant for their effectiveness. However, just like the PwC case above, large-scale redesign of executive positions is not within the domain of coaching. Instead, coaches help coachees delegate better and prioritize to deal with overload issues. Decision-making skills like those are important for leadership effectiveness and can impact the business if applied the right way.

Coaches also help their coachees' motivation, giving them tools to cope with stress and make better career choices. That can improve business results if the executives' energy is focused properly.

The deepest insights provided by the analysis came in the area of individual capability. Coaches often focus the work with their coachees based on 360 assessments of the executives' leadership behaviors. Those usually are drawn from competency models that are supposed to measure the behaviors that differentiate top from average leaders.

The interview analysis found that it often is very hard to make a link between the focus of coaching and specific business impacts. One reason is that leaders usually indirectly impact business results through their team's work, not directly through their own actions. A second reason is that the leadership competencies are not always what is needed in some contexts to improve strategy execution and organizational effectiveness. For example, communication skills can be important, but they may make a material difference only in rare situations when there is a true crisis. Coaching the leader's team members can help their professional development but have little impact on the bottom line. And so on.

The insights from the Strategic Analytics diagnostic pointed to context as critically important for whether coaching positively impacts the business. The coachees' role demands, their team's needs, the specific business challenges they faced, and so on created unique circumstances in each case. For any competency to have a business impact, the key factor is knowing when and how to apply it. In most cases, improving leadership competencies had no impact on the business. In the cases where it did, there was a specific barrier to improved business performance that a particular competency enabled the executive to overcome.

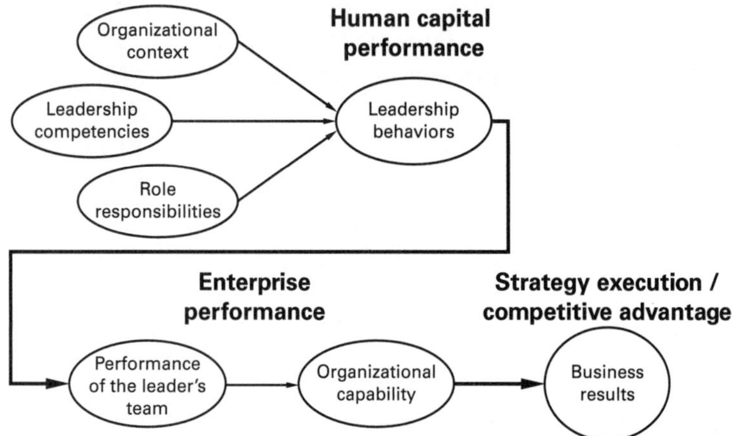

Figure 13: Causal Model for Evaluating the Business Impact of Executive Coaching

Figure 13 shows the causal model for evaluating the business impact of executive coaching. Note that performance of the leader's team (under Enterprise Performance in the bottom of the figure) depends on many more factors than just the leader. A more complete model of enterprise performance would include those other factors as well. Figure 13 excludes those factors only to focus attention on the role that the leader plays; it is not a complete depiction of how an executive's team achieves business results.

Analyses at Both the Enterprise and Human Capital Levels

The most complete systems diagnostics involve in-depth analysis at both the enterprise and human capital levels. When there are sufficient time and resources, this approach can yield the deepest insights for improving strategy execution and organization effectiveness. The two case studies below provide examples of the kinds of insights they can deliver.

A complete systems diagnostic takes the longest time and the most resources to complete. It typically requires a cross-functional team capable of doing the analysis at both the enterprise and human capital levels. The full systems diagnostic can be applied to a wide range of issues. However, given the time, energy, and resources required, I have found that these diagnostics are usually applied to issues that are at the core of an organization's competitive advantage, involving people and processes that are central to executing the organization's strategy. This is the case for two reasons.

First, the stakes are higher for those kinds of issues than in other cases, for they have the greatest potential to impact the organization's operations either positively or negatively. Doing the complete diagnostic maximizes the likelihood that subsequent decisions will have the biggest impact on strategy execution. Senior leaders are willing to invest the resources necessary for doing the full diagnostic in cases like that.

Second, the time needed to complete the diagnostic means the insights provided need to be worth the wait. Senior leaders often have the most patience when the issues are critically important to strategic success. They may not be willing to wait for in-depth analysis of issues that are only tangentially related to the organization's core operations.

A key concern is whether previous attempts have been made to address the issues in question. When you're talking about a company's main operations, many core issues around productivity, motivation, and morale are perennial. They persist from year to year, despite multiple attempts by both business leaders and HR to solve them. Lasting solutions usually are lacking because a non-integrated analytical approach is used by both groups. A Strategic Analytics diagnostic almost always can identify the perennial problems' causes and effective solutions.

There's one final note before we get into the details of the case studies. What's important to understand about conducting the diagnostic is that "system" means a complete set of business processes that address a particular aspect of strategy execution. The specific focus in any situation depends on the business challenge to be addressed. In the route sales case study, the company wanted to improve productivity on the routes, so that was the focus of the enterprise analysis. Under other circumstances that same company could have used the Strategic Analytics diagnostic for other business challenges, such as productivity of their manufacturing operations. The business unit optimization case study focused on the business unit design for a professional services company. In other settings the focus could have been customer satisfaction with specific client engagements for that same company. The case studies provide just two examples of the many different focuses the enterprise analysis can take as part of a complete Strategic Analytics diagnostic.

Case study 5: Route sales maximization. Frito-Lay, a division of PepsiCo, uses a direct store delivery (DSD) system to sell the majority of its products. In that kind of system, Frito-Lay's own employees are responsible for getting the product to the stores (driving and delivery tasks), putting it on the shelves and rotating the stock (merchandising tasks), as well as negotiating with the store manager for additional display space (sales tasks). For more details on this case study, see Levenson and Faber (2009) and chapter 9.

In a DSD system, routes are constructed to optimize the use of the delivery truck and the route sales representative's (RSR) time. In Frito-Lay's case, this meant creating two main route types: high-volume routes with larger trucks that were used daily to serve a small number of high-volume stores like Wal-Mart and large grocery stores, along with low-volume routes with smaller trucks, a much larger number of stores, and less frequent delivery schedules. The RSR on a low-volume route is the only person who interfaces with the store. On a high-volume route, national sales teams and regional account teams work directly with the retailers' corporate offices on many aspects of promotions and product mix, leaving less leeway for the RSR to influence sales at stores.

Step 1: Identify the sources of competitive advantage and where the problems are. Competitive advantage in mass-market consumer products like the ones Frito-Lay produces comes from having marketing, sales, and distribution systems that enable large volumes of goods to be sold at relatively low prices (as compared to say, automobiles and other high-price, low-volume products). When the strategy is executed well, large market shares can be gained and maintained, producing healthy profits. In the DSD system, the RSR contributes to strategy execution by maximizing the volume of products that are sold, using the individual's time and the truck assigned to the route.

At the time of the case study, there were three issues of concern for Frito-Lay: RSR compensation, which had fallen behind the company's local benchmarks for target compensation in some regions; turnover of longer-tenured RSRs, which they thought might be due to compensation; and ways to increase productivity from the RSRs' time on the routes and from the trucks. Longer-tenured RSRs are more productive, so the concern was that the compensation gaps might negatively impact route sales.

Data for the case study came from a number of different sources, including RSR and supervisor interviews and surveys, as well as route performance data for the RSRs that were matched to their survey responses for analysis.

Step 2: Enterprise analytics. The organizational design was the main focus of the enterprise analytics. The design and staffing of the routes were examined for potential productivity improvements. Other DSD companies separated the three parts of the job so that they were performed by different people, usually having one person do the driving and delivery, and the merchandising, and having another do the sales tasks. Frito-Lay was considering breaking the tasks into separate roles on the high-volume routes to make better use of the RSRs' time.

It was determined that neither the culture nor core organizational capability needed to be tweaked because they already provided strong support for Frito-Lay's strategy. The culture had a very strong orientation toward effective execution, which aligned well with the demands of running a consumer products company that manufactures and distributes massive quantities of goods. The DSD system was a large part of the core of that organizational capability, which the potential organization design changes were supposed to support directly.

The analysis revealed that on the high-volume routes, the RSRs' ability to meet tight delivery windows on all stores on a route was a bottleneck to performance. The solution was to assign more merchandiser help to those routes. That freed up the RSRs to spend more time doing driving and delivery, enabling more stores to be added to existing routes. This made better use of the RSRs' time while increasing utilization of truck capacity.

Step 3: Human capital analytics. The human capital analytics focused on compensation's role in driving turnover and productivity, and the importance of specific skills for route sales.

An analysis found that regions with low compensation had higher turnover for shorter-tenured RSRs; there was no relationship with longer-tenured RSR turnover. So fixing compensation

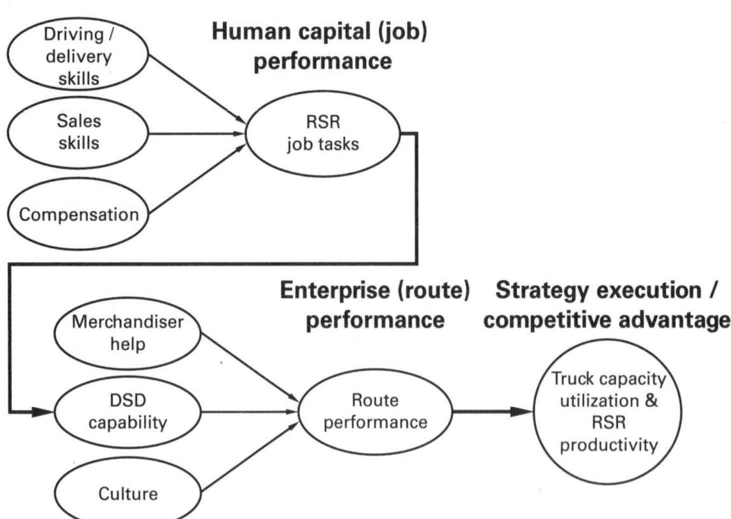

Figure 14: Causal Model for Route Sales Maximization

in those regions helped with retention of low-tenured RSRs, but not with retaining the more productive, longer-tenured RSRs.

Analysis of the RSRs' prior experience before joining Frito-Lay found that those with more sales experience had greater route sales. And despite the importance of the driving and delivery tasks on the high-volume routes, greater prior sales experience positively impacted sales on both route types. Those results further supported assigning more merchandisers to the high-volume routes—it freed up the RSRs to spend more time on both sales tasks and driving and delivery tasks. Figure 14 shows the causal model for this case study.

Case study 6: Business unit optimization. The senior leaders of a professional services firm were concerned that many locations had grown so large they had become hard to manage. Leadership wanted to improve both client service and employee utilization by restructuring offices into smaller business units with fewer clients and employees.

Step 1: Identify the sources of competitive advantage and where the problems are. In many offices the number of employees had grown to be very large. The firm found that there was a divide between the management of its top versus average employees that had potentially negative impacts on client service. The top employees were perpetually in demand, worked on a large number of engagements, and received a disproportionate share of the more desirable assignments. Senior leaders wanted only the best people on their teams and lobbied hard to get those employees on their engagements.

As a result, the top employees were stretched thin by working on too many engagements, while the utilization rate of the average employees was below the firm's targets. This dynamic was perpetuated by the unequal access to important developmental experiences, which were much more readily available to the top employees. So the average employees had fewer opportunities to build critical skills to make themselves more valuable for future engagements. Senior leaders had little incentive to solve the problem, because they were held accountable predominantly for client deliverables, not for ensuring everyone had suitable skill development and work experiences.

The organizational redesign that the firm launched created smaller business units within the large offices. Each unit had a relatively small number of senior leaders and enough employees to service the client engagements of those leaders. In addition to the traditional responsibility for serving their individual clients, the senior leaders within each business unit were held collectively accountable for financial performance across all the clients and for utilization of all employees in the business unit. Dedicated HR representatives assigned to the business units helped ensure that all employees received career planning and developmental experiences to boost client engagement skills.

The analytics assessed the success of the new business units by using a combination of interviews of both leaders and employees, surveys of both groups, and linked financial and utilization data.

Step 2: Enterprise analytics. The enterprise analytics matched measures of group effectiveness to business unit performance. The measures of group effectiveness helped determine if the business unit leadership worked well together, creating an effective teaming environment for the employees. The measures included shared understanding about the BU's goals and methods for achieving them, along with commitment to the BU. Parallel measures of the employees' shared understanding and commitment to their client engagements were also collected.

The analysis found a relationship between the measures of BU group effectiveness and the BU financial outcomes and employee utilization. This validated the senior leadership's decision to create the new BUs, demonstrating the business case for them. Further evidence came from an analysis that showed a link between the BU's measures of group effectiveness and the measures of client engagement effectiveness; this meant that each leader's own client engagements benefited from being part of the larger BU. These two results helped the senior leadership

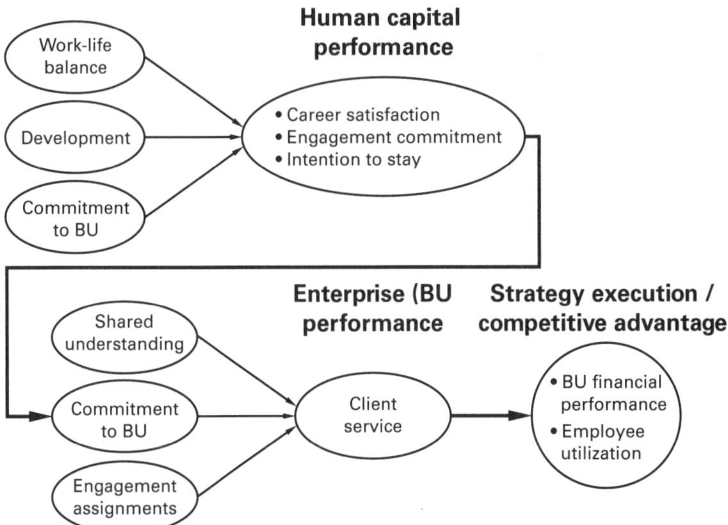

Figure 15: Causal Model for Business Unit Optimization

persuade reluctant BU leaders that the new organization design was in their own best interests.

Step 3: Human capital analytics. Measures of employee motivation and wellbeing were analyzed and linked to their BU commitment and client engagement commitment. The analysis revealed that employees' intention to stay with the firm and their career satisfaction were both positively impacted by their commitment to their BU and to their client engagements. This provided further evidence to reluctant BU leaders of the value of the new design: it increased retention and motivation of the talent they needed to serve their clients.

A very strong link between work-life balance and development support and the employee outcome measures (intention to stay; career satisfaction) supported the firm's goals of ensuring that all employees, not just the top performers, were served well by the new design. The emphasis on better career development through assignment of client engagements and balancing the work load across all employees resulted in greater employee career satisfaction and improved work-life balance.

The causal model for the business unit optimization case study is summarized in figure 15. Only some of the elements of the full causal model are represented in the figure. The complete analysis incorporated four different models: (a) factors leading to business unit performance, (b) factors leading to client engagement performance, (c) the relationship between business unit and client engagement factors, and (d) factors leading to human capital performance.

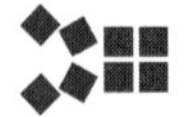

Chapter 8

Application—Customer Retention and Profitable Growth

Issues Addressed in This Chapter

- Case study examples of Strategic Analytics applied to the dual strategic objectives of customer retention and profitable growth
- Examples provided for commercial banking, technology companies, and retail sales companies

Key Questions

- What specific strategic objectives are we trying to accomplish when we target profitable growth?
- Which operational metrics do we need to diagnose problems with profitable growth?

The case studies in the previous chapter showed that the details of Strategic Analytics depend on the business context and strategy. Since the analytics focus on the factors that create competitive advantage (chapter 4), it makes perfect sense that the details vary from one case to another.

The next two chapters delve deeper into that point. They show how the same strategic objective often translates into different measurements and issues to address, depending on the company's context and sources of competitive advantage. This chapter addresses customer retention and profitable growth. The next chapter covers go-to-market strategies.

Customer retention is a primary objective for all businesses. Despite that universal objective, its meaning and relationship to profitable growth vary greatly. Consider first the example of large commercial banks.

- **Strategic objectives:** For banks, customer retention and profitable growth means growing total assets under management, increasing margins by optimizing the mix of deposit and loan instruments, and minimizing customer turnover to reduce deposit acquisition (marketing) costs.
- **Enterprise elements needed to execute the strategy:** The enterprise elements (capability, organizational design and processes) needed to execute the strategy include product innovation, cross-selling, a robust regional or national network of branches and ATMs, extensive online banking options, and highly personalized customer service for the very profitable clients with high net worth. The customer service strategy includes cultivating ties with clients having lower net worth who are likely to become more wealthy.
- **Competitive advantage analytics:** The first analytic step analyzes how effective the bank is at each strategic objective: which ones need the most attention, and what actions are needed to accomplish them. For example, total assets under management may be growing quickly, but with the "wrong" mix of deposit and loan instruments, leading margins to erode.

Possible causes	Potential solution
a. The market for higher-priced loan products is saturated, eroding overall margins	Product innovation and / or expansion into higher-margin lines of business
b. Increased competition for deposits has driven up interest rates and liabilities costs	Market research / intelligence on competitors' sources of deposits
c. A spurt of asset manager hiring increased the proportion of lower ability asset managers	Improve asset manager screening and training
d. Lax frontline management led to decreased accountability for hitting product mix targets	Improve asset manager performance management

Table 4: Possible Causes and Solutions for Changing Bank Deposit and Liability Mix

Senior leaders often rush decisions about issues like the instrument mix problem because they focus almost exclusively on quarterly results. When presented with a set of possible causes and solutions like those in table 4, most leaders settle on one of them and push their direct reports to fix the perceived problem without a lot of additional analysis.

These senior leaders often will do simple analysis, such as looking at current data relative to historical trends. For example, a slowdown in the rate of sales of higher margin products, compared to the prior year, supports the first possible cause—a saturated market for those products. Yet it also supports the fourth one as well—lax management of asset managers, which led them to focus less on higher margin products.

Competitive advantage analytics addresses the possible causes in table 4. Evaluating the solutions' likelihood of success requires both enterprise and human capital analytics. Not having both produces a gap that leads to incomplete diagnosis.

The place to start for enterprise analytics is the strengths and weaknesses of the organization (table 5). These include the

Organizational strengths	Diagnostic questions
a. Safety of assets	• How can the bank's reputation be leveraged for greater attraction and retention of customers? • How can the reputation be enhanced to improve the brand?
b. Breadth of branch and ATM networks	• How do customers use local access points to engage with the bank's services? • How is the demand for electronic banking and mobile options changing how the bank has to provide a full spectrum of access options?
c. One-stop shop for most financial services	• How is the mix of products customers use evolving away from the bank's traditional portfolio of offerings? • What capabilities need to be built, and what behaviors have to change, to address that evolution?
Organizational weaknesses	**Diagnostic questions**
d. Impersonality	• How to improve the customers' experiences when they interact with employees and technology systems?
e. Lack of agility to adapt to innovation from more focused, narrow businesses and from nonbank competitors (e.g., mutual fund companies; on-line mortgage lenders; wealth management firms; and others)	• How to improve speed of responsiveness?

Table 5: Diagnostic Questions to Ask for a Bank's Organizational Strengths and Weaknesses

strengths of asset safety, network breadth, and one-stop shopping, while the weaknesses are impersonality and lack of agility. For each strength and weakness, table 5 provides sample diagnostic questions that lower-level HR and frontline managers can use to identify areas of improvement that support strategy execution and organizational effectiveness.

The analysis has to be guided by the economic realities of how the strategy can be accomplished. For example, improving the quality of customer interactions can increase customer retention. If HR and local managers follow that mandate without analyzing the impact of their actions, they might design training so that local branch personnel spend more time working with every client. The training would improve the quality of customer interactions. However, not all customers contribute equally to the bottom line. The customer acquisition and retention cost has to be weighed against the benefit of a specific customer's financial assets.

Understanding the economics of that relationship is critical. For the large number of low- to moderate-income customers served by a bank—people with at most a mortgage and relatively small amount of nonretirement savings—there is a limit on how much the bank can afford to invest in making their experience less impersonal: the benefit of additional assets from these customers is small. The solution for them is interacting with local branch representatives and call centers, with no individual representative personally assigned to their account. Headcount levels are balanced to manage wait times and can be minimized by encouraging greater use of ATMs and online transactions.

For wealthy clients, in contrast, the potential benefit of additional assets is enormous. In order to attract and retain these clients, the bank structures the work design very differently. Account management teams work with small groups of clients. This creates a highly personal experience, the polar opposite of the more impersonal experience of lower-income clients, and very different priorities for HR and local managers. Adding more local branch staff to attract and retain lower-income clients usually cannot be justified, because the additional labor costs exceed the benefits of the additional deposits. The situation for clients with high net worth is the opposite: if the account management teams are sufficiently productive, the bank can add as many personnel as needed to provide personalized customer service. The investment extends to training as well: if some account team personnel have competency gaps that reduce effective team functioning and customer service, it's usually financially worthwhile to close those gaps.

The group that provides perhaps the greatest challenge from an analytics standpoint is the clients who have higher incomes but are not wealthy. Senior leaders know this group is important for two reasons. The bank can make money providing financial services based on their current wealth, and they have the potential to become high net worth clients in the future. The challenge is how to make these customers' interactions with the bank less impersonal than those of lower-income clients but not as high touch as the high net worth clients' interactions. The solution involves customer service at a cost between what is spent on the lower-income and high net worth clients.

The task for Strategic Analytics is to first build a causal model showing the impact of individual capability, team effectiveness, and customer interactions on client retention (like the examples in chapter 7). Then the model can be tested to see how the work design and budgeting decisions made by senior leaders impact the different factors that contribute to client retention.

Customer retention and profitable growth for technology companies. In contrast with commercial banks, technology companies rely on profitable innovation and network effects for customer retention and profitable growth. Innovation keeps them at the forefront of the competition, providing cutting-edge products that attract new customers at the right price points. Network effects mean that larger bases of consumers or businesses using a product attract others to use it. This leads to more companies providing ancillary products and services, and more users providing peer support on using the product.

The specific capabilities needed for profitable innovation vary across technology companies. At the height of their success in the 1990s, Microsoft and Intel prospered together by creating an operating system, processor, and suite of software applications that worked together very well. Intel provided the processor innovation, relying on the capability enabled by hardware engineers, manufacturing and quality experts, and supply chain specialists who determined the best locations and methods of production around the globe. Microsoft provided the software and operating system innovation, relying on software engineers to write the code and create a community of developers beyond Microsoft that created a more robust suite of applications. Microsoft also relied on corporate sales and support functions that kept their fingers on the pulses of corporate IT departments. This helped ensure that the products met the purchasing managers' needs at the right price points.

During this same period, IBM and Oracle also targeted corporate IT departments but with different approaches. IBM focused primarily on hardware sales—everything from mainframes and servers to desktop computers. Oracle built its business on database software and multiyear licensing contracts. For both companies, in contrast with Microsoft and Intel, technical support provided after the initial sale played a much more important role in customer retention and future sales. Thus, the organizational capabilities needed to support customer retention and profitable growth for these four companies had very significant differences due to their different business models.

When it came to their weaknesses, all four companies shared a blind spot related to the evolution of the Internet. Microsoft and Intel relied too long on the desktop and laptop markets, missing first the emergence of Internet searches (Google) and then the move to Internet-based services and mobile-based applications. IBM was eclipsed by Cisco in providing the hardware backbone for routing Internet traffic. Oracle only very recently has started to address delivering software as a service over the Internet; IBM similarly is now pushing hard into cloud-based computing.

Microsoft was late to recognize the importance of Internet-based computing. Once they realized the strategic importance of the Internet, the subsequent challenges were due to failures in strategy execution. Microsoft tried to catch up with Google's search engine but was never able to close the gap: they were too oriented toward their strengths in operating systems and desktop/laptop computing. They did not focus enough on how to overcome their weakness in search and in ad-based revenue streams (versus license or subscription-based revenue streams, which were more lucrative).

The key question is whether Microsoft's structure and processes prevented them from closing the gap in search faster. By many accounts, their Bing search engine ultimately equaled the technical capabilities of Google's search engine. However, the lengthy time needed to close that gap enabled Google to develop a dominant share in search, including a successful ad-based revenue model.

The standard diagnosis of strategic failure in this case would highlight that Microsoft's DNA as a company was strongly oriented toward a business model based on operating system and software sales, not on searching and display ads. Despite that orientation, Microsoft's strategy to be a leading platform for Internet activity likely was the right one. The task for Strategic Analytics in this case is to determine what aspects of Microsoft's organizational design, culture, rewards, and so on were more strongly aligned with its traditional business model of operating system and software sales, and what aspects were sufficiently aligned with the emerging model of Internet-based activity. In retrospect, had Microsoft earlier recognized the fundamental shift toward Internet and mobile computing, they would have proactively changed more of their design, capabilities, and culture at the enterprise level and reinforced that move by aligned changes in design, capabilities, and attitudes at the human capital level.

A related issue, highlighted by Apple's success, is how technology companies should strike the right balance between emphasizing technical features only versus emphasizing technical features plus industrial design. Many engineering-oriented technology companies focus on the technical aspects of the product first and the consumer experience second, if at all. Steve Jobs historically was given the lion's share of credit for Apple's success in creating so many winning consumer products (iPod, iPhone, iPad, iTunes, and others). Yet integrating industrial design principles into a technology company's DNA cannot be mandated from the top, even when the CEO is Steve Jobs. It requires hiring people with those capabilities, providing the right rewards for incorporating industrial design principles into R&D and manufacturing processes, and orienting processes toward the industrial design approach.

For technology companies operating in the consumer hardware space, analytics of an industrial design strategy would examine:

- Is the design of the organization and of individual roles consistent with a primary emphasis on industrial design principles?
- At the enterprise level, do the industrial design organizational capabilities compete with capabilities that support a different approach?
- Is the organization's culture sufficiently oriented toward industrial design? Do performance management and rewards support the industrial design strategy?
- Do the people have sufficient industrial design capability? Do they prioritize industrial design when doing their work?

For technology companies whose strategy is to focus more on Internet- and mobile-based computing, all the analytics diagnostic questions above apply equally if you substitute "Internet computing" or "mobile-based computing" wherever "industrial design" appears.

Customer retention and profitable growth for retail sales companies. For companies that rely on retail sales made directly to the public, employee satisfaction and engagement can drive customer retention and increased sales. This has been an accepted "fact" for years since the highly publicized case studies at Sears and other companies (see, for example, Heskett, Sasser, and Schlesinger, 1997, and Rucci, Kim, and Quinn, 1998). Thus it would seem reasonable to have a strategy of increasing employee engagement. Applying Strategic Analytics shows how that strategy depends on the role.

Competitive advantage analytics first identify the role that different jobs play in promoting customer retention. The impact varies a lot from role to role. Only employees with roles having direct public contact in sales and customer service can singlehandedly impact the customer positively or negatively. A salesperson can help sway a customer to purchase more items at higher prices. A customer service representative can make a customer feel special and think that the company cares about him/her, or a bad representative can have the opposite effect, driving the customer into the arms of a competitor.

The other jobs support the employees in the public-facing roles. Greater employee engagement in the support roles might lead them to provide better service to the frontline employees. However, even if the supporting role employees in finance, logistics, building maintenance, and others enthusiastically do their jobs, that can have minimal impact on customer service. If the customer service representatives are lackluster in their customer interactions, customer retention can still falter.

Strategic Analytics highlights that the people most directly in contact with customers have the greatest potential to impact retention. They are the most direct transmission mechanism from employee engagement to customer retention. The further away from direct transmission a person or role is, the smaller the impact of their engagement on customer retention.

This has direct implications for the relationship between employee engagement initiatives and customer retention in retail sales organizations. To maximize retention, the initiative should more narrowly focus on the customer-facing roles. Improving employee engagement in non-customer-facing roles may contribute, but it has to be evaluated relative to other potential improvements in the work design and capabilities. That is the task for Strategic Analytics.

One final point about competitive advantage analytics: not all retail sales transactions benefit from increased employee engagement (see Chapter 2 for further discussion). The key is the value proposition of the customer interaction. To be specific, ask "what draws the customer to our products," "what features are they looking for," and "how can we get them to see greater value in buying more from us?" For more expensive discretionary items, enticing the customer to linger enables selling them additional products; Nordstroms and retailers of luxury goods use this exact strategy.

Starbucks is another example: highly engaged baristas make the customers feel welcome, encourage multi-item sales, and soften resistance to paying more for coffee and food than other retailers charge. The higher prices are justified in part by better quality, but the products do not sell themselves. The barista's job is partly to convey the value of their higher-quality coffee, tea, and food.

These cases support the conclusion that employee engagement can drive profitable growth. In contrast, in many other types of retail transactions, the value proposition is low prices and/or speed of the interaction. At gas stations and convenience stores, customers who purchase food and coffee don't want the high-touch, high-quality Starbucks experience. They are content with cheap coffee and "good enough" food delivered by efficient service that gets them in and out of the establishment as quickly as possible.

At Wal-Mart the customer value proposition is the lowest prices; at Target and CostCo it is low prices for higher-quality items. For all three retailers, it does not help their strategy to train store personnel to spend their time talking with customers so they linger longer: customers aren't looking for that type of interaction. In these retailers' systems, investing additional resources in headcount yields a better return when applied to critical functions like purchasing, supply chain management, and marketing, and to roles in local stores that enable greater volumes of goods to be sold while minimizing inventory levels. More personnel roaming the aisles talking to customers is not a justified expense.

Supporting higher margin sales with more highly skilled employees through high-performance work design is covered further in chapter 10.

Chapter 9

Application— Go-to-Market Strategies and Effectiveness

Issues Addressed in This Chapter

- Case study examples of Strategic Analytics applied to go-to-market strategy effectiveness
- Incorporating the people element into work design based on operational objectives
- Minimizing labor costs while maintaining organizational capability

Key Questions

- How can we strike the right balance between technical excellence within a business unit or function, and cross-functional collaboration?
- How can we maximize capacity utilization while accounting for employee discretion in deciding which processes to follow precisely?

A company's go-to-market (GTM) strategy is how it delivers its products and services. A robust GTM strategy includes price and margin targets, the delivery systems, and links back to the operations. The functions responsible for GTM typically include sales, marketing, and some variant on product management (product development and/or manufacturing).

The entire GTM process is highly complex. The sales function is in charge of pricing and sometimes also final-stage delivery of the product. The marketing team makes advertising and brand management decisions, often sharing some customer outreach responsibilities with sales. The product management/operations group creates the products and services under the cost and quality objectives.

The biggest challenge facing GTM systems is achieving the right degree of coordination among the different components. If the marketing team creates a new way to draw customers in, the sales and product management teams have to deal with the new customers. If the sales team wants higher volumes through reduced pricing, the product management team has to fulfill the new demand. The product management team needs continuous sales updates for supply chain management.

Inefficient management of the GTM system often is a prime source of strategy execution failure, which makes it a good candidate for applying Strategic Analytics. In fact, poor integration often directly contributes to GTM systems problems. This chapter addresses a number of the Strategic Analytics issues involved with GTM systems.

Designing GTM systems for technical excellence versus cross-functional effectiveness. As Adam Smith first noted, specialization of labor is the foundation of economic growth. Henry Ford commercialized the principles with the modern manufacturing line. Specialization is a foundation of modern organization design but so, too, are the cross-functional collaboration challenges. These challenges have direct implications for the effectiveness of GTM systems.

Specialization leads separate functions to be responsible for different technical competencies: marketing, sales, manufacturing, customer service, finance, HR, IT, and so on. Having those dedicated functions avoids reinventing the wheel for functionally specific tasks.

Having standalone functions solves the technical efficiency problem while simultaneously creating coordination problems across functions. The solutions range from matrix organization designs to team-based organization designs. Under a matrix design (Galbraith, 2009), centralized functions maintain (shared) direct control over the processes on which they are experts. Under a team-based organization design (Mohrman, Cohen, and Mohrman, 1995), functional experts work within cross-functional teams and report primarily into those teams.

The problem is that matrix organization designs are no guarantee that GTM systems will be effective, especially when three or more functions are involved. The first focus for Strategic Analytics is the reporting relationships and mechanisms for cross-functional collaboration. How effectively do sales, marketing, and product management come together to make pricing, production, distribution, and marketing decisions? Do they put the enterprise's interests ahead of their function's more narrow objectives? What are the criteria for GTM decisions?

Technical-only versus technical-plus-people work design. A second problem in GTM systems design is incorporating the perspectives of the people who do the work. Most work systems are designed by strategic, financial, or technical experts who are removed from the work. People experts are often excluded from many design decisions. Processes are designed one way initially but evolve over time. Process innovations frequently are not documented or become part of the tacit knowledge about how work gets done. Thus the financial/technical experts miss key parts of what happens and why.

As Lawler and Worley (2011) explain, there have been two dominant approaches to work design since the dawn of the industrial age. The traditional command-and-control approach focuses on the work tasks and ignores the characteristics and needs of the people. It combines close employee monitoring with managers making all key decisions. The traditional manufacturing line is a classic example: narrow jobs and small spans of managerial control that facilitate close monitoring.

The other approach comes out of the sociotechnical systems approach, sometimes called the high-involvement approach; Beer (2009) calls it high commitment and high performance. This approach acknowledges people's creativity and innovation: if managed the right way, they can promote competitive advantage. It emphasizes communication transparency and frontline employee decision making. Team-based manufacturing lines are classic examples. Many professional services and consulting companies use high-performance organizing principles.

Chapter 10 addresses the aspects of high-performance work design on which Strategic Analytics can help shed light. For the current discussion of GTM systems, the key is that companies can decide between more narrow, tightly controlled jobs, versus broader jobs with greater information sharing and decision-making authority. The Strategic Analytics task is to examine whether the work design, information sharing, and decision rights are aligned properly. For example, do salespeople identify information from customer interactions to improve pricing and contracting? Does that information benefit the bottom line? Do product management employees help improve production and distribution processes? Is customer intelligence quickly reported to product management and marketing? Are sales and marketing integrated into product development and management decisions?

Most organizational design decisions are made solely at the senior executive level. Therefore frontline managers and HR professionals do not get to decide between command-and-control versus high-performance work design. However, because GTM systems are so complex, the analytics needs to focus on work design. If you are in charge of diagnosing the sources of your GTM system challenges, it is your duty to examine work design issues even if you were not specifically asked to do so. It is much better to ask for forgiveness than permission. If you apply Strategic Analytics, you are much more likely to identify the true causes of performance shortfalls.

Minimizing labor costs while maintaining capability. Minimizing costs while maintaining capability in GTM systems is challenging. When a GTM system is working well, short-term financial goals are often met through budget cuts. In the very short term, minor budget cuts in compensation, employee development, capital improvements, and other areas never have an immediate negative impact on the effectiveness of GTM systems. If we reduce spending on employees, equipment, or buildings by a few percentage points today, how will that materially impact the business over the next quarter? The answer: not at all. Even over a longer term, a one-time small budget cut will not have a material impact on performance. So managers have a strong incentive to meet short-term financial goals by shaving budgets wherever possible.

Since a one-time small budget cut has no big performance impact, there is an enormous temptation to continually make small budget cuts to meet short-term financial goals. Ultimately this strategy will backfire, because capability will start degrading. So the short-term balanced budget goal and the longer-term competitive advantage goal are in conflict.

For example, as detailed in chapter 7, Frito-Lay at one point gave control over the labor budget to regional GTM leaders (Levenson and Faber, 2009). Over an extended period, they underinvested in frontline employee compensation, creating large gaps between target and actual compensation in some locations. The result was higher turnover and lower capability among the people who stayed.

When a company underinvests in plant and equipment, usually the negative impacts on productivity can easily be traced back to the underspending. The negative impacts of underinvesting in people, in contrast, are harder to detect initially. In Frito-Lay's case it was years before slowly trimmed labor budgets led to increased turnover and reduced productivity. Even then, people knew that there was a potential compensation problem but couldn't validate its role relative to other causes. A Strategic Analytics diagnostic was needed to find multiple causal factors: compensation plus other solutions.

Maximizing capacity utilization and distribution system efficiency. Maximizing capacity utilization is a key operational objective for GTM systems. When factories, warehouses, and trucks are used at capacity, capital cost per unit sold is minimized.

The challenge is that many different processes, functions and frontline roles contribute to capacity utilization. Consider two different GTM systems, both of which use delivery trucks: the package delivery industry's GTM system, and consumer products companies' direct-store-delivery (DSD) system. In both cases, maximizing capacity means optimally using the storage volume on the trucks and minimizing distance and time driven to save fuel and labor costs. How that plays out in the two different industries is quite different.

Consider first package delivery and logistics companies such as UPS and FedEx. Maximizing use of capacity for these companies in part means maximizing the volume of and prices charged for packages. This includes both outbound packages from the distribution centers and inbound packages the drivers pick up from customers.

Including package pickup makes the optimization equations much more difficult to solve than outbound deliveries only. Other factors include drop box availability and other businesses that receive packages for shipment for the company. The latter can be critical for GTM success, which is why FedEx and UPS acquired Kinkos and Mail Boxes Etc., respectively. Those acquisitions bolstered their customers' options and relieved some of their drivers' package pickup volume.

The challenge for GTM system designers is that employee discretion can subvert route optimization. The employees have to know and embrace their roles as ambassadors for the company when interacting with customers. They need to balance giving the customer what she wants and optimizing total time on the route. What is the right decision when you have just delivered a package to an address and the customer asks you to wait while he retrieves a different package to ship? How long do you wait? Is it better to leave without the package, incurring the cost of an angry customer to keep the schedule intact?

The GTM system designers have to conduct Strategic Analytics that include truck time and distance driven, individual differences in how drivers react to job duties, and the cost-benefit ratio of increasing system capacity. The human capital part of the analysis covers how employees respond when they have discretion over customer interactions, the skills needed for those interactions, and the labor cost of those skills. The enterprise part of the analysis covers the organizational design and labor costs for alternative package intake options (drop boxes and business pickup locations).

Consider now consumer products DSD systems. Under a DSD system, one person is responsible for transporting the product from the company's warehouse to the retailer's store, merchandising the product in the store, and negotiating additional display space. The consumer products DSD role has many of the same responsibilities as the package delivery and logistics role: driving, unloading packages/boxes, and interacting with the customer. There also are significant differences. The DSD driver merchandises the product on the retail store's shelves and bargains with the store for additional display space. Even though the driver has no control over pricing, the job directly impacts sales via ordering and keeping the shelves stocked with the right product mix, and acquiring additional display space in key store locations.

Optimizing use of capacity includes the choice of delivery truck and many other factors. Dedicated merchandisers may be employed to provide help on the route, freeing up the driver to focus on delivery and sales tasks. Some products may be shipped through a warehouse system instead: the products are then delivered to the retail stores through a separate channel, and the retail stores handle merchandising. The decisions over additional merchandisers and which products to send through the DSD system depend on both technical factors and driver motivation and capability.

Strategic Analytics needs to diagnose the drivers of motivation and productivity for the core DSD tasks. This means analyzing the core tasks that are hard to monitor, such as the effort expended to make the sales pitch to the grocery store manager for additional display space. That incentive challenge is a main reason why DSD drivers are typically paid on commission. Yet commission-based pay does not ensure employees will always make decisions that are completely aligned with what the company wants to achieve. Strategic Analytics must address how employee psychology interacts with the work design to generate the behaviors observed on the job.

Part III

Diving Deeper: How to Make Current Practice Better

The three chapters in this last part of the book cover a range of topics related to the current practice of analytics in organizations. In some cases the Strategic Analytics approach is a critique of current practice, so there are improvements that can be made. In other cases, the discussion provides additional detail to help you apply Strategic Analytics in ways that might not be immediately obvious from the content in Parts I and II.

Chapter 10 covers a number of issues related to critical roles, competencies and performance. Topics include measuring top talent and high potentials, diagnosing if jobs are designed the right way to deliver high performance, and the value of measuring commonly used leadership competencies.

Chapter 11 addresses the insights available from sensing data and the dangers of taking a too-narrow approach. Sensing data on organizational structures and people processes need to be interpreted within the larger context of the system and desired strategic objectives.

Chapter 12 discusses how to evaluate human capital development. The traditional build versus buy decision is addressed, along with an alternative approach—redesign.

The final chapter concludes with key learning and action points from the book.

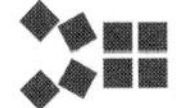

Chapter 10

Critical Roles, Competencies, and Performance

Issues Addressed in This Chapter

- Measuring top talent and high potentials
- Diagnosing if jobs are designed the right way to deliver high performance
- Critical roles and competencies versus organizational capabilities

Key Questions

- How does the contribution of individuals contribute to performance of the group?
- What is the right balance between focusing on individual-level versus group-level metrics and performance?
- What role do leaders play to enable the group to perform?
- How do we know that jobs are designed and compensated the right way to deliver high performance?

This chapter addresses a number of topics related to performance. High performance is a goal that organizations always strive for. The multiple ways of addressing it include identifying top talent, nurturing individuals with high potential, focusing on critical roles, and paying special attention to leadership. The chapter uses the Strategic Analytics approach to evaluate common practice in each case.

Top talent, high-potential people, and critical roles are important and therefore these roles and people should deserve special attention. But what does that mean in practice? Top talent and high potentials are supposed to be the best performers today or have the potential to develop into top performers. We need to know how they contribute to leverage and maximize their contribution.

For critical roles, a key question is whether business performance depends on the role alone or on a group of roles acting together. This question is frequently ignored in the discussion of critical roles. However, it is essential to understanding how to improve performance. Focusing on only one role can miss the larger picture of how the group collectively helps execute the strategy.

There's a related challenge with leadership. Enormous attention is paid to leadership's potential impact on organizational performance, but not enough is focused on system design. In most cases, system improvements should precede or accompany focusing on individual leaders.

The chapter concludes with a discussion of high-performance work design. If there is too much attention paid to identifying important individuals or roles, the opposite is true for the principles of job design. Organizations everywhere routinely experiment with job design, but do not necessarily follow principles that have been widely established as effective. Applying Strategic Analytics the right way includes knowing the tradeoffs involved in pursuing high-performance work design. In cases where the work design is suboptimal, there usually is substantial room for increases in productivity and organizational effectiveness.

Identifying top talent and high potentials. Identifying and cultivating high-potential employees is an obsession in many companies. We often hear statistics like only 20% of employees deliver 80% of performance or 20% of customers are responsible for 80% of total sales. Those figures come from research showing that a relatively small group of people typically are responsible for a disproportionate percentage of total performance, output, or sales. The 80–20 "rule" that gets bandied about is catchy, though it has hardly been proven across all organizations and work processes; in fact, the variety of work settings that have been tested is very small (O'Boyle and Aguinis, 2012). Nonetheless, the idea that a small number of employees are disproportionately responsible for organizational performance is both a common perception and one that can make logical sense as well.

Everyone has seen the outstanding individual performers who more than carry their own weight in producing organizational results—the superstars. Sometimes these are "pros in position": professionals who are expected to remain in their roles indefinitely because they are highly productive where they are, and both they and the organization are happy with them doing that job for a long time. Others are rising stars, who are expected to move onto larger and more challenging roles. There is no question that all organizations have these highly talented people working for them. The real question is what analytics can tell us their existence means for strategy execution and organizational effectiveness.

To start, it would be extremely helpful to identify who these people are, and this is where the first challenge arises. Research has shown consistently that promoting someone solely on the basis of past performance is often a recipe for disaster: you may be taking people who are highly capable of doing their current jobs and thrusting them into situations where they will be mediocre at best. Experience is the best teacher and the best screener: when people have realistic job previews, where they can try out (parts of) the job before taking it on fully, the information revealed is extremely useful. It is useful to the people being considered for the role, because they get to see how they feel about the new tasks; it also helps the organization to see them perform and determine if they are more or less likely to succeed in the new role.

Organizations often rank early-career people on the basis of potential, but the science behind those ratings is often questionable because they are not based on realistic job previews. People who are considered to have high potential often get greater access to developmental opportunities and challenging assignments that are not provided to others. There is nothing wrong with this strategy in theory, but a key point should be recognized. Given that experience is the best way of developing most competencies, if the people considered to have high potential are given a very different set of developmental experiences, the high potential program could become a self-fulfilling prophecy: the people considered to have high potential ultimately succeed precisely because they received that designation.

There may be nothing wrong with taking the high potential approach; it is just important to recognize the likely sources of success. If the source is the experiences the high potentials receive, then great care should be taken to analyze and understand what they learn from those experiences, the kinds of competencies built through them, and how that ultimately enables them to support the organization's effectiveness and execution of its strategy. Taking a scientific approach to understand how those competencies are developed and deployed successfully will ensure the best use of available resources, and may expand the range of people considered to have high potential.

There is another key point about individual contribution that needs to be taken into account. Even if it is true that the superstars account for a disproportionately large portion of value created for the enterprise, what are the implications of that? Does that mean we should focus on hiring only superstars and/or devoting the lion's share of organizational resources to support them? In most cases the answer is no, but you need to apply Strategic Analytics to determine exactly what should happen.

Consider the role of superstars in the overall picture of organizational performance. Operations are optimized by matching people with the right set of skills to a particular set of tasks. Not all tasks require the highest level of skills: the economics of maximizing total profit earned requires making money off activities ranging from those with lower cost/lower productivity to higher cost/higher productivity ones, with different sets of people doing the different types of task. Recall our discussion of the sources of competitive advantage in chapter 4; see also the section on high-performance work design later in this chapter. Only some jobs and tasks require the higher productivity workers who also cost more. Strategy execution and organizational effectiveness can be achieved through having lower-priced talent in many roles.

The notion that we should cater to the superstars because they are top performers misses the point about optimizing the system and performance. Some people and roles are higher investment/higher productivity, while others are lower investment/lower productivity. You need both to serve the complete range of customers you have: every business has some higher margin, more critical customers and a larger group of lower-profit customers from whom you can still make decent money. Moreover, there are limits on how much you can afford to spend even on superstars: they provide a net benefit only if their productivity is sufficiently high to make the higher costs incurred to employ them worthwhile; if they are too expensive, it can be more profitable to do without them.

Critical roles. When organizations aren't focusing on the contributions of individual employees, they often focus on trying to identify critical roles. The belief is that if certain roles are more important for strategic success, then they deserve extra attention to ensure strategy execution.

The central question is how to define critical. Do you define it based on the job's role in strategy execution? Everyone agrees that scientists are essential to the R&D process at pharmaceutical companies, that marketers are essential to business success at consumer products companies, and that computer technology companies cannot do without software engineers. Organizations already pay a huge amount of attention to such core roles. There is little benefit to designating them as critical because they are already viewed that way.

Part of what can make a role critical may be the challenges created by a vacancy of more than a very short period of time. If a long-term vacancy would be very disruptive, then that certainly implies that the role is critical. The more important question for Strategic Analytics is not whether a vacancy would be disruptive, but how difficult it would be to fill the vacancy via the talent supply chain.

The first question is how easily the role can be filled by internal promotions or external hires. If there is a readily available supply of people who can step in, then that lowers the criticality of a vacancy. A second consideration is the amount of time it takes a new person to get up to full productivity in the role. If there is a steep learning curve, that makes the role more critical: even if you can fill a vacancy quickly, the hit to productivity while the new person gets acclimated raises the cost of a vacancy.

A third consideration is whether a tweak to the work design could lower the criticality of a vacancy. Can the team members be cross-trained to step in for each other whenever there is a vacancy? Cross-training does not solve the problem of finding a replacement in the long term, but it can greatly lower the cost of short-term vacancies. And having a cross-trained team can make the transition of a new person much easier: the entire team can help with onboarding, shortening the time needed to attain full productivity.

A role can also be critical if improving it would aid strategy execution. Recall the discussion of the average productivity or contribution of a role versus the improvement in performance available from making a change to the role (chapter 5). Productivity often can be increased more by investing in roles that traditionally have been under-resourced because their average contribution is lower than other roles.

Individual versus group performance. HR systems are designed to select, evaluate, reward, and promote people on the basis of their individual competencies and contributions. When we look for the sources of organizational performance or failure, it is natural to look for heroes and goats—the individuals who deserve special praise or blame.

In order to understand how an individual role contributes to performance, a critical piece of information is the interdependencies of the role. Interdependencies tell us the extent that organizational performance is generated by the independent, unrelated actions of individuals acting on their own versus in coordinated and interdependent ways with other roles and people. Recall our discussion in chapter 1 of the contributions to strategy execution that come predominantly from roles acting independently. Only certain jobs in functions like sales and customer service carry that distinction; everything else of value for our customers is created by the interdependent actions of people in groups or teams.

Interdependency among roles creates a challenge for organization design and HR program design. To maximize collective accountability, you need to ensure that each person in the group is individually accountable for their contribution. Yet when the work is highly interdependent, focusing exclusively on individual accountability can ignore the integration among team members that is critical for group success.

Consider a new product development team like the Boeing 787 Dreamliner discussed in chapter 11. Each person on the team has an essential role to play in the team's success. Yet the team is successful only when the contributions of each person are integrated and aligned with the group's objectives. No one person can be held accountable for the integration. Technically, the team's leader is ultimately responsible for integration, but in reality she (or he) can only guarantee the integrity of the integration oversight process, not the integration itself—that requires the willing contribution of the team members who have to do the actual integrating of their own work into the work of their teammates. In the case of the Dreamliner, there were many, many different sub-teams responsible for different parts of the airplane's development, manufacturing, and assembly. Each sub-team had very specific, measurable objectives that required all members of the sub-team to do their jobs and that required their work to integrate seamlessly.

The task for Strategic Analytics is to examine the work system and interdependencies among the roles, along the lines described in chapters 5 and 6: how effectively do the team members coordinate and integrate their work? The role of the performance management and rewards systems should be examined in detail. Given the usual overemphasis on individual-level accountabilities, performance management, and rewards, a prime candidate for improvement is often a greater emphasis on group-level accountabilities, performance management, and rewards.

Leadership competencies and effectiveness. The use of leadership competency models in organizations is extremely popular. Having a competency model for leadership provides the impression that there is a scientific basis for evaluating leaders. However, there is virtually no proven link between leadership competency models and improved strategy execution and organizational effectiveness.

The first big problem is that the models focus only on observed behaviors, not critical skills like decision-making ability. The observed behaviors are related to organizational performance but are incomplete at best. As Drucker (1967) pointed out years ago, leadership competency is largely about effective decision making. However, that kind of skill can't be easily measured like other leadership behaviors that are commonly part of 360 evaluations today.

The competencies included in the typical models can contribute to strategy execution and organizational effectiveness; see the discussion of evaluating the impact of executive coaching in chapter 7 for details. However, there is little concrete evidence they do so, in part because the behaviors are fairly benign. The behaviors usually are the minimum criteria for being a good manager or leader: without them the person likely would be ineffective, but they are not sufficient to differentiate contributions that directly support strategy execution.

Judging by the amount of time, energy, and resources devoted to leadership development and compensation, a casual observer could easily conclude that leaders create the greatest value for an organization. That of course is an overly simplistic conclusion: leaders rarely do anything on their own to create the products and services that customers purchase. They do make critical strategic and operational decisions every day, but the success of the organization depends as much or more on the work that is performed by others following those decisions—the work that enables the strategy to be accomplished.

The other big problem with leadership competency models is that they focus too much on individual leader behaviors and not enough on good group processes and dynamics. Group dynamics measures usually are excluded because the leader cannot directly control them. Yet they are essential contributors to strategy execution. A better approach to leadership competency starts with group dynamics measures (chapter 5), and links those to the desired organizational capabilities.

As example of this is the case study in Levenson, Van der Stede, and Cohen (2006). In that case a company redesigned the work in its manufacturing operations, moving from a traditional, hierarchical command-and-control approach to more self-directed work teams. The company's strategy was to use the self-directed teams to improve frontline decision making, avoiding the extra time needed when decisions are elevated up the chain of command, ultimately improving the quality of the products produced in the facilities. The new approach also enabled a reduction in the number of middle managers and an increase in their span of control, since they could spend less time micromanaging the frontline workers.

As part of the move, the company introduced a managerial competency model that reflected the managerial skills consistent with the new work design. Key new skills included managing through influence (as opposed to command-and-control), along with coaching and developing their direct reports to perform their expanded duties. The end result was improved organizational performance that was partly due to the new managerial competencies.

The skills emphasized in this case are ones that appear in many leadership competency models. However, this case is the exception that helps prove the rule. There was a direct link between the managerial competencies and organizational performance: the managerial competencies were a necessary part of what the teams needed under the new work design (self-directed decision making), which was a core part of the company's strategy. In most other cases, no such direct link exists between leadership competencies and organizational performance, and thus there is little to no bottom-line justification for specific leadership competency models.

High-performance work design. For over a century, starting with Frederick Taylor's scientific management, Henry Ford and the birth of the manufacturing line, organizations have experimented with restructuring work to increase productivity. Job design for the first half of the twentieth century focused on making jobs narrow so they could be performed easily by people with low levels of education. The second half of the twentieth century saw improvement on that approach: organizations used job enrichment, job involvement, high-performance work design, and semi-autonomous and self-managing work teams to boost productivity. High-performance work design offers the promise of greater productivity and process improvements by involving employees in the work in a way ignored by traditional, narrowly-defined jobs. To achieve high-performance work design, you need to avoid simplified jobs and to design enriched jobs as much as possible (Lawler, 2003).

The key to maximizing performance across the entire organization is finding the right mix of narrow versus enriched jobs. Today both the principles of scientific management and the principles of high-involvement work are alive and well, and they often operate under the same roof. Call center representatives, route delivery drivers, data entry operators, fast-food workers and many more jobs show the hallmark of scientific management, with scripted routines to minimize deviations from established processes. At the same time, many other jobs, especially knowledge-intensive professional and technical jobs, fit the classic definition of enriched jobs: they have a lot of variety, autonomy, and decision-making authority.

Taylor's scientific management approach designs jobs to be simple and narrow so they can be performed by people with low skill levels. The classic example is the dull, boring, and repetitive assembly-line job. The negative consequences of simplified jobs are low intrinsic motivation, high turnover and absenteeism, and greater risk of unionization. Enriched jobs, in contrast, provide more intrinsic motivation by allowing the workers to feel they are accomplishing something with the work (meaningfulness), to see that they are responsible for the outcomes of the work, and to receive feedback or knowledge of the results. When these conditions hold, employees are much more likely to care about the quality of work, take ownership over what they are doing, and willingly offer ideas on how to make improvements in work processes.

A key aspect of high-performance work design is that decision-making power is moved downward in the hierarchy. Giving frontline employees greater decision-making authority and autonomy is a core part of high-performance design, because it makes them responsible for the outcomes of the work. Having decision making authority and the desire to be given credit for proper decision making are both important drivers of motivation to perform at the highest levels possible.

Recall our discussion in chapter 4 about the sources of your organization's competitive advantage. Some organizational processes are more critical for competitive advantage, while others are not. High-performance work design is more cost effective when used for jobs that directly contribute to competitive advantage; however, there is not a strict one-to-one relationship. You need to apply analytics first to understand the logic of the jobs' designs, and then examine whether the actual design and behaviors are consistent with what is needed for successful strategy execution.

Sometimes high-performance work design means that for some people jobs are enriched, while other people who work next to them do not have enriched jobs. Consider the case of a corporate headquarters. Many of the jobs at headquarters are enriched: senior leaders and most of the professional and technical people who report into them have jobs with considerable decision-making authority and autonomy. Other headquarters jobs, such as those of the janitors or food-service workers, typically are not enriched. These workers have more tightly prescribed rules, little authority to make independent decisions, and strong supervisor oversight.

As a contrast, consider now the workers at a manufacturing plant that produces components for high-end electronics, run by companies such as Intel, Qualcomm, and Samsung. The products in these plants are often produced in clean-room environments: the risk to the quality of the products from even minute amounts of dirt or dust is extremely high. The janitors who work closest to the clean rooms can have a direct and very negative impact on the quality of the products being produced. So their jobs are given greater responsibility as part of the site's strategy to maintain the integrity of the clean-room environment. The office headquarters janitors, in contrast, do not play such a critical role: if they fail to do their jobs properly, the headquarters offices will be dirtier than they should be, but the negative consequences are typically minor at worst. Similarly, food-service workers at the manufacturing plant have no bigger role in creating competitive advantage there than they do at headquarters, so their jobs should not be designed for high-performance in either location.

In what settings would food-service workers play a more strategic role? An obvious place is very high-end restaurants. Though the job generally speaking is the same—preparing food to be served to customers—the contribution to the organization's strategy and competitive advantage is very large at high-end restaurants. In settings where food service quality does not strongly and directly contribute to competitive advantage, like office buildings and manufacturing plants, the job design can be more traditional, narrow, and not enriched.

The principles of high-performance work design have been adopted in many settings across numerous industries. Yet despite the promise of greater productivity under high-performance work design, the complexity of executing all the elements of the design often leads to results below expectations. Even if the design is absolutely the right choice from a strategic perspective, if it is not performing as expected there is going to be a lot of uncertainty regarding the sources of poor performance. If you see things not working well, did that happen because a high-performance design was the right choice but not implemented well, or did it happen because it was the wrong choice in the first place? The analytics must address both these issues at the same time, which means examining the current work system for flaws in design.

Applying Strategic Analytics in this type of case means examining the design of the work system to determine where the barriers to better performance reside. Consider, for example, the role of managers in high performance work systems.

Managerial behaviors in a high-performance work system. In a high-performance work system, frontline employees have a greater deal of autonomy and decision-making authority compared to those in more traditional, narrow jobs. One way high-performance work systems achieve greater productivity is through reduced numbers of managers and greater spans of control for them. The other is through quicker problem solving at the point where the work is performed—the frontline workers. This means managers in a high-performance work system do more coaching and less micromanaging, both because they are supposed to and because they have less time for micromanaging, given the greater spans.

The different managerial behaviors extend to proactive, transparent communication and two-way feedback as well. Proactive, transparent communication is necessary so that the workers are well-informed about what is happening in the business, why it is happening, and how their actions impact the business processes and objectives. Two-way feedback is needed so that the workers feel comfortable speaking openly and honestly about issues they see that need to be addressed. In response to the upward feedback, their supervisors must not just listen but also take action either to make changes or to explain why change is inappropriate or infeasible.

All these features of managerial behavior in a high-performance work system are prime candidates for analysis. Are the workers getting the information they need to solve problems effectively? Are they given the autonomy to solve the problems? Are they micromanaged? Are they getting sufficient training and coaching to close the skills gap? Are leaders managing multiple levels down because of problems with past performance or lack of trust that the frontline employees can do the work on their own?

Compensation design and competencies for high performance. When frontline workers are given greater autonomy and decision-making responsibility under a high-performance work design, they need skills to manage the greater challenges and job demands. People who have greater autonomy and decision-making authority need the ability to make the right decisions. The expectations for higher productivity come at a price, though. Higher compensation typically is needed to attract and retain the kinds of people needed to do the work. So you have to have proper alignment between the work design and the compensation design. Table 6 shows where the two are aligned versus not.

Many perceived problems with employee motivation can be traced to compensation design that is not aligned with the work design. The desire to squeeze labor costs while maintaining expectations for high productivity often leads the compensation design to lag behind the work design; the Frito-Lay case discussed in chapter 7 is one example. The problems arise when there are mismatches: high compensation with low skills (overpaying) or low compensation with high skills (underpaying). Underpaying is more common and comes from focusing too much on "where can we save money" and not thinking enough

Work design and compensation design have to be aligned for maximum effectiveness		Expected productivity	
		Lower	Higher
Compensation design	Higher	**Not aligned**	Aligned
	Lower	Aligned	**Not aligned**

Table 6: Align Compensation and Work Design

about how to maintain and build strategic capability. The end result is that employees are unmotivated and unproductive because they don't see enough rewards for the heavy demands placed on them. Overpaying, where it exists, often happens when a strong general manager fights for the "highest quality" people—the A players—in every role in his/her organization when B players may be all that is needed in some roles for effective strategy execution.

A prime target for Strategic Analytics is examining the role of the compensation system in attracting, retaining, and motivating the employees needed to execute the strategy. This includes starting with the organization capabilities needed to realize the strategy (chapter 4), and investigating the role of compensation and other job design factors (chapters 5 and 6).

Chapter 11

Making Sense of Sensing Data

Issues Addressed in This Chapter

- Pros and cons of using sensing data to diagnose strategy execution challenges
- Aligning metrics on organization processes with strategic objectives
- Making a culture more innovative

Key Questions

- When do diminishing marginal returns for a sensing metric kick in—when can you have too much of a good thing?
- What actions can be based on employee survey ratings of organizational processes? What other information is needed to make sense of them?
- Where does culture take organizational processes so far that strategy execution is impeded?
- What does it mean to be more innovative with existing processes versus challenging entire business models?

This chapter addresses how to make the best use of sensing data on your organization design and people processes. Some of these data are direct measurements, such as headcount, spans of control, ratios (such as number of employees per HR person), safety incidents, time to hire, vacancies, and so on. Others are survey-based employee ratings of organizational processes, behaviors, and culture.

Sensing data play a very prominent role in evaluations of organizational performance and strategy execution for two reasons. First, they are one of the few ways to determine whether many organizational processes are operating as they should. Second, they are often used for benchmarking against other organizations. They are both essential and misused at the same time.

You can't live without them, you can't live with (only) them. Sensing data play a central role in any Strategic Analytics evaluation. Consider the case study examples in chapter 7. The 360 data that inform leadership competency models are sensing data on individual behaviors. The time RSRs spend driving versus in store are sensing data for Frito-Lay on DSD system performance. The number of support function employees in headquarters versus business unit roles is sensing data on appropriate organization design. Turnover rates are sensing data for PwC on key talent retention. And so on. Each of these types of sensing data provides a critical insight into understanding if the organization structure is correct and whether behaviors and processes are consistent with strategic objectives.

While sensing data play an important role, they also are often misused when viewed out of context. Leaders love to benchmark, which is how they evaluate operational performance. Benchmark data on quality, margins, market share, customer satisfaction, and other areas are essential for measuring strategy execution. Many consulting companies collect sensing data from competitors in the same industry and sell the aggregated benchmark data back to those same companies for comparison.

The risk, as we discussed in chapter 4, is that there are limits to how zealously (and reliably) any one benchmark can be used to measure strategy execution. There is a cost-benefit consideration to making improvements along any one dimension. At some point diminishing marginal returns dictate that you stop pushing for more. In addition, organizational design choices make direct comparison of even "objective" data—headcount ratios, time to complete tasks, and others—hard to interpret out of context.

For example, you may have more HR people per employee than your competitors, but if your HR people are more directly engaged in supporting competitive advantage, the extra expense could be well worth it. Alternatively, they might be doing little to add value to the bottom line, in which case the higher headcount might not be worth it.

Cost-benefit tradeoffs in organizational effectiveness mean that benchmark data on organizational design and people processes are rarely useful when considered in isolation. What is the right level of turnover? Are there optimal headcount ratios? Is there such thing as "enough" of a leadership behavior? When are spans of control too narrow or too broad? And so on. In each case, the answer is that it depends on the other objectives you are trying to accomplish. Reaching the right conclusion requires additional data and deep knowledge of the context. You have to look at the bigger picture of what's going on in the system.

The rest of the chapter addresses this issue in more detail, with specific examples on safety data, speed of decision making, and making a culture more innovative.

Safety data. Safety data are a classic example of something that at first glance appears to be unequivocally good. However, there can be too much emphasis on safety, as discussed in chapter 3.

There are diminishing marginal returns even for safety improvements. One company I worked with was fanatical about safety—for good reason. They operated dangerous equipment that could kill or maim people if not handled properly. So a laser-like focus on safety was definitely warranted.

However, their emphasis on safety at times went a little too far. Some leaders concluded that using a metric around safety incidents was the best way to ensure all opportunities for improving safety were maximized. Any site with safety incidents had to report them to a central location, and the local managers' performance evaluation depended on having as few incidents as possible.

The problem was that the system did not differentiate readily between minor incidents (a stubbed toe leading to a small fracture, a finger caught in a door while it was closing, and similar cases) and more egregious cases where life and limb were truly in jeopardy. The end result was that local management often had to do quarterly fire drills to try to increase their safety rating even when the only incidents were minor ones. The organization gained a benefit from driving toward zero safety incidents for major accidents, but not from trying to eliminate minor bumps and scrapes that can never be eradicated completely. The organization had failed to do a proper cost-benefit assessment of driving all safety incidents to zero.

Speed of decision making. For another example, consider the case study from chapter 7 on speed of decision making. In that case, the company used a benchmarking service provided by a consulting company that surveyed its employees about a number of organizational processes.

The benchmarking data raised concern about decision making speed. Being in the pharmaceutical/biotech/medical devices industry, the company knew the value of being careful and deliberate in making key product decisions. If more time and data were needed to make sure a product was safe, the company would readily do what was needed. In that sense, taking a long time to make certain business decisions was a good thing, and leadership knew it.

What concerned them was that they rated low relative to their peers in the industry on decision making speed. They also knew that their consensus-based culture could slow things down. These two reasons together caused them to question whether decision making was too slow.

Applying Strategic Analytics led to the root cause of slow decision making—unclear decision rights (as detailed in chapter 7). However, the benchmark sensing data alone were insufficient to get to the root cause. Additional data on the organization structure and processes were needed to make the definitive determination.

Making a culture more innovative. In this last example we will address making a culture more innovative. In this case, like the previous one, a company had concerns about the efficiency and effectiveness of its processes. Leadership knew the company had to become more innovative but struggled to articulate precisely what that meant for people in different roles.

The challenge they had was twofold. They knew they had to get better at dealing with innovations that threatened to change the fundamental nature of their business—disruptive innovations that could reinvent entire business models. In addition, they also had concerns about how tightly controlled their internal processes were. They wanted to get better at being innovative with their day-to-day processes so they could more easily make adjustments when they were needed to improve organizational effectiveness.

As it turned out, the issues involved were quite different for these two different types of innovation: disruptive innovation versus process innovation. The rest of the chapter covers these two examples in depth.

Disruptive innovations present fundamental changes to business models, threatening existing revenue streams and often forcing large-scale reorganization for successful adaptation. Process innovations are changes to existing processes to make them more efficient and effective; process innovations can range from changes requiring only minor tweaks to the organizational design to those requiring large scale redesign. The mechanics of making disruptive innovations work generally are much more difficult than process innovations. Both types of innovation require organizations and their leaders to think outside the box—figure out how to do things differently to maintain and grow the business.

Disruptive innovation. Disruptive innovation is the holy grail of corporate strategists: figuring out how and where the current successful business model is going to be upended by new products, services, and technologies is an obsession in board rooms and C-suites around the world. I do not have a solution to make the ideation process more efficient and effective. However, Strategic Analytics can help assess strengths and weaknesses in innovation that are related to the organizational design and culture.

Industry	Disruptive innovation	Organizational response
Music	Digital music files shared over the Internet	New business model
Utilities (electricity generation)	Home-based solar panels; distributed / customer-based generation	New generation and distribution strategies
Biotech	Biosimilars (generics)	Greater integration of branded and generic business models
Airplanes	Composite materials	New manufacturing and assembly processes

Table 7: Sample Disruptive Innovations and Organizational Responses

To start, consider the examples of disruptive innovation and organizational responses in table 7. The move from songs distributed via albums and CDs to digital files freely shared over the Internet totally upended the existing business model for music companies. Electric utilities face major disruptions to the economics of their existing business model as house-top solar panels reduce demand for traditional electrical power and increase the opportunity for distributed electricity generation and transmission. The traditional separation between branded pharmaceutical companies versus generic drug manufacturers may be upended in biotech: the greater complexity of producing generics (biosimilars) in biotech means greater margins, larger barriers to entry, and a much stronger argument for one organization to produce both branded and generic products. The introduction of composite materials for the body of large aircraft required the introduction of new manufacturing and assembly processes.

The very nature of disruptive innovations means that adapting your organization to deal with them involves changing large parts of the design, capabilities, and culture, including performance management and rewards criteria. The problem is that it is very difficult to make those changes in an organization that is already optimized for your current, successful lines of business without creating major disruptions to ongoing operations.

Current operations are highly optimized. We know exactly what it takes to get the work done—how many people, what occurs at each stage of the process, likely variances in output and the reasons for them, and other issues. Prospective operations, in contrast, have a great deal of uncertainty. Until the new way of working has been tried and optimized over a significant period of time, there is no way of mastering all the variables to be managed and different operating problems that will pop up.

This chicken-versus-egg problem creates a budgeting challenge: how much should be invested in the prospective new business? It is easy for the general managers of ongoing operations to make sound ROI arguments for increased spending in their operations. They have lots of data to analyze and support their plans. For general managers of new operations that haven't been optimized yet, the uncertainty makes forecasting very difficult.

During the initial forecast of what the organization's structure, staffing, and processes will look like, the tendency is always to underestimate the resources needed. One reason is the unforeseen risks of the new venture. Identifying all likely scenarios and variances is too cumbersome for planning purposes. A reasonable number of scenarios are considered, a preliminary budget is made based on those, and the work is started.

Only after the work is underway is the uncertainty resolved. Inevitably, additional expenditures are needed to deal with unexpected scenarios. We can call this tendency to underpredict operational problems the uncertainty planning bias.

The other reason is the competition for funds with the existing "cash cow" lines of business. All general managers (GMs) are competing for the same limited pool of funds to run their business, even if they have full profit and loss (P&L) responsibility for the business they manage. In order for the GM of the new venture to get funding approval, it always helps to have a more optimistic projection of costs, revenues, and the time needed to generate healthy profits. We can call this the funding forecast bias.

The uncertainty planning bias and the funding forecast bias together ensure that virtually every new venture that is launched in organizations around the world takes longer to accomplish its goals, usually with very large budget overruns. Consider, for example, Boeing's development of the 787 Dreamliner airplane. The Dreamliner's innovation was a much more extensive use (50%) of composite materials than had ever been done before in a large body airplane. This required major reworking of the manufacturing and assembly processes.

There was enough prior history of composite materials' use in airplanes and other applications that Boeing could forecast with a high degree of certainty that the materials would work. What was uncertain was how much work would be needed to sort everything out. Under construction of a traditional metal frame airplane, such as the Boeing 747, there are 1 million holes drilled in the fuselage during assembly. By substituting a fuselage made largely of composite materials, the 787 has fewer than 10,000 holes in the fuselage.

As disruptive innovations go, introducing composite materials that extensively into airplane design was a significant change in traditional procedures, but not a fundamental change in the business of aircraft design and manufacturing. It should have been easier for Boeing to forecast how long developing the new plane would take and how much money it would cost compared to new ventures in other industries that are more disruptive of traditional manufacturing models. Despite that, the development of the 787 Dreamliner took much longer than Boeing had anticipated and at much greater cost than initially planned—undoubtedly because of uncertainty planning bias, funding forecast bias, and the challenges of introducing new processes in an organization well versed in doing things a different way.

My purpose in highlighting the challenges Boeing encountered with this moderate innovation in airplane design is to emphasize how uncertainty creates problems in both the planning and execution phases of the new strategy. The job for Strategic Analytics is to diagnose how success can be improved through shortened development time and/or lower expenditures. The following are a set of issues to be addressed through the analytics, with examples of the questions to answer in each case.

- **Allocation of decision rights/annual budgeting and strategy setting:** The analytics should look for evidence that (a) the new venture is not independent enough from existing operations or (b) has been underfunded or is being managed with less urgency and focus than if it were a standalone company focusing only on the new venture. How committed is the organization to making the new venture work? Who carries ultimate decision-making authority over the new venture? Can they be vetoed by decision makers running the traditional "cash cow" businesses, which compete with the new venture for funding? How much investment is leadership willing to make in the new venture? Is the new venture being treated as something that has to succeed no matter what, even if there are cost overruns and anticipated revenue falls short over the short to medium term?
- **Criteria for determining success:** What are the strategic and financial metrics used to determine success of the new venture? Do the criteria for those metrics conflict with the traditional measures used to determine strategic and financial success for your current organizational

processes (margins, volume, type of customer, and so on)? What operational metrics do you use to determine if you have developed "enough" of the organizational capability needed to make the new venture a success?

- **Culture:** What parts of the culture are aligned with the new business and which ones are in conflict? You need to make sure that the design criteria and work processes are carefully monitored to minimize culture's negative impacts on the new venture.
- **Role competencies:** You need to find the right mix of new hires versus reassigning current employees to work on the new venture. Reassigned people provide the necessary link back to the current organization and "how things get done." New hires can bring state-of-the-art knowledge on what is happening externally with the new market developments. They also don't suffer from allegiance to the old way of doing things. Communication and decision rights among the two groups have to be carefully balanced to ensure both perspectives receive enough weight. The role for analytics is to look at the team composition and dynamics and determine their role in achieving the business' desired strategic outcomes.
- **Performance management and rewards:** Getting the right mix of performance management and rewards at the individual role level can be difficult. People who work in emerging industries or market segments often enjoy much greater autonomy than people who work in large organizations—there are fewer control mechanisms. Many of them enjoy working in more entrepreneurial environments. Given those differences, what will it take to get people like that to come work for your venture? The entire performance management and rewards system can't be remade to fit the needs of the new venture, so the organization may need to carve out something different and unique for the people working on the new venture. That creates transition issues.

What do you do with people if it doesn't work out? It is better to deal with those issues after the fact if the venture doesn't succeed than set it up for failure at the front end by not getting the initial conditions right.

Another task for analytics is examining people's motivation. Which aspects of the existing performance management and rewards are consistent with the expectations of external people who are immersed in the development of the new business in other organizations? What kinds of career paths do they face externally versus internally? What signals are being sent to internal people who decide to work in the new venture? The signal that says "go do this assignment and if you pay your dues you can come back to what you were doing before" is a very different signal than the one saying "this is a critical task we have to solve for the future of the company." Executives who have tied their careers to an internal path may be too risk averse to take the risks needed in the new venture.

In Boeing's case there was a lot that did not change about the basic strategy and organizational design: they were an airplane designer and manufacturer before the use of composite materials, and that did not change materially after they introduced composites in the 787. The fundamentals of what a large body airplane is did not change: the physics and aerodynamic principles that dictated the basic shape and functioning of an airplane were not changed by introducing more composites. "All" that happened was that Boeing introduced a new type of material to the production process. So it was a much less disruptive innovation than often is the case. This was not like the music industry that saw its profit margins disintegrate with the move from CD distribution to digital; it was more like the move from vinyl albums to CDs.

Despite a moderate degree of disruption, in the Boeing Dreamliner case a lot still went wrong with the execution. Why were they ultimately successful where other companies have come up short? One important reason is they went all-in: they didn't give themselves other options and committed to making the new process work. They were not successful in the short term: it took much longer and cost more than originally forecasted. This is precisely why they are a good case study of some of the challenges of implementing a new organization design in the face of disruptive innovation.

Senior leaders often believe they have no choice but to pursue disruptive innovations, with all the challenges they bring for strategy execution. Strategic Analytics cannot solve the fundamental organization design problems that are created by that strategy. It can help diagnose the sources and some solutions for those challenges.

Process innovation. Process innovation is very different from disruptive innovation because it addresses the efficiency and effectiveness of existing work processes. Any organizational or work process can be addressed by process innovation. Examples include call center operations, claims processing, procurement procedures, manufacturing processes, customer relations, distribution systems, supply chain operations, and many, many more. Process innovations improve the efficiency and effectiveness of processes that are defined by the existing strategy and organization design.

The idea of process innovation is not new: it includes approaches such as the learning organization, continuous improvement, and Six Sigma. The issue I address here is not how to identify process innovations, which is the focus of those types of initiatives, but instead how to identify the organizational design components that can prevent process innovation initiatives from being effective.

The challenges of getting process innovations to stick arise from the same issues that bedevil disruptive innovations: in order for existing processes to be efficient and effective, they have to be tightly optimized so that there is little deviation from established best practice. Getting the organization system to switch away from established best practice can be difficult unless there is a culture of constantly challenging existing practice and encouraging people to contribute useful ideas.

The larger issue is providing sufficient incentives so that the people who are best positioned to make improvement suggestions will do so voluntarily. The employees who are involved in the day-to-day work often have important insights into ways to improve work processes. Some of them are happy to make process improvement suggestions with the simple reward of seeing their ideas put into practice. Others need a different motivation such as being rewarded for making suggestions. Solutions to that problem range from introducing gain-sharing compensation programs (Mulvey and Ledford, 2002) to (re)designing the entire work system using high-performance design principles (chapter 10).

The problem with asking frontline employees to provide process innovation suggestions is the benefit, or lack thereof, that accrues to the employees from doing so. Some people are motivated simply by the desire to help the company improve and achieve its goals. Some are motivated to contribute by the potential for future rewards through promotion and career advancement. Many other employees are not necessarily motivated to contribute voluntarily but also are not opposed to doing it, so long as it does not cause negative repercussions for themselves.

For example, none of the following typically have any negative repercussions for frontline employees: improving manufacturing line product quality, reducing supply chain or post-production inventory, and reducing inefficient materials and equipment usage. Improving the ergonomics of work stations can improve productivity by reducing injury time spent on medical leave of absence. Yet other productivity improvements can be viewed negatively by frontline employees.

The classic conundrum for frontline employees who have insights into productivity improvements is the downside risk to their personal workload and compensation from making suggestions. If they point out ways to speed up the work with the existing headcount, their workloads will increase. If they find more efficient ways to do a given set of tasks, freeing up their time, the company likely will find additional things for them to do, expanding the scope of their responsibilities. At the extreme, if the suggestions conserve a large amount of labor input time, some employees' jobs could even be eliminated. When the company responds to productivity improvements by increasing the job demands, it is called ratcheting up the job requirements. When employees anticipate that response and proactively hold back on identifying and suggesting productivity innovations, it is called a ratchet response.

Concerns about the company ratcheting up the job requirements are why many employees need to see tangible benefits from making productivity improvement suggestions. This is where solutions such as gain-sharing and no-layoff policies can be important: they enable the employees who make the productivity innovation suggestions to share in the financial benefits generated by those improvements without fear of working themselves out of a job. Doing so can greatly reduce ratchet effects. Lincoln Electric is a well-documented example of a successful gain-sharing approach to compensation and work design, and by far it is not the only success story.

The task for Strategic Analytics is to examine the work system, the types of process innovations the company wants to achieve, and whether the work system's features are inconsistent with promoting employee-generated process innovation suggestions. How do the different employee segments feel about making voluntary suggestions? Are they worried about negative repercussions? What steps has management taken to reassure them, and do the employees believe that messaging?

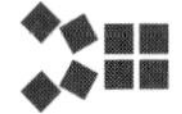

Chapter 12

Evaluating Human Capital Development: Build versus Buy versus Redesign

Issues addressed in this chapter

- Analyzing the impact of training and development—challenges with the Kirkpatrick model
- Training and development as standalone interventions or part of larger integrated solutions
- The build versus buy versus redesign decision for critical skills

Key questions

- Can the ROI of training be measured on its own?
- When is combining training and development with other interventions most effective?
- Is it better to develop from within or hire externally? Would you get better organizational outcomes if you considered changes to the work design?

One of the most critical issues facing organizations is how to build the individual-level capabilities required for executing a strategy. Are the competencies of people currently in the roles the right ones to ensure strategy execution? How do we know if our efforts to build talent contribute to effective strategy execution?

Chapter 10 addressed the issue of identifying critical competencies and how they contribute to group performance. In this chapter I discuss how to use Strategic Analytics to evaluate the development and retention of individual skills. The first part of the chapter, which addresses training and development, draws from Levenson (2014b). The second part covers the build versus buy decision.

Evaluating program design versus intent. A key issue in evaluating an HR program is whether you evaluate the program's design or its intent. For example, merit raises are supposed to motivate people to perform. The design goal of the program is to differentiate compensation based on performance, which is one target measurement. The program's intent—providing increased motivation to perform—is separate and much more difficult to measure.

For training and development (T&D), the intent is to increase organizational capability. The program design is to do it through individually-focused skill building. Kirkpatrick's (2006) four steps model for T&D evaluation, which is widely used, is a classic example that focuses mostly on program design, not intent.

There are four steps in the Kirkpatrick model: (1) measure the learners' reactions to the T&D program; (2) show that learning occurred and that skills were developed; (3) show application of the learning on the job; and (4) demonstrate business impact. People who apply the Kirkpatrick model almost never get to business impact because they get bogged down with steps 2 and 3 and because it can be very difficult to show a direct link to business impact.

The logic behind the steps of the Kirkpatrick model is quite compelling. If it is possible to complete each step, then it is very easy to conclude that the T&D program had the intended impact and can be given credit for positively contributing to business performance. If evidence of positive results from one of the steps is lacking, then the role of the T&D program can be called into question.

For example, if the learners like the program (step 1) but it cannot be shown that they have learned the skills (step 2), then the program may never have built the skills as intended. If the intended learning occurred but is not applied on the job (step 3), then the skills might not be useful from the learners' perspective. Finally, if learning occurred and is applied on the job but there is no positive business impact (step 4), then the program likely provides no additional value. The logic of the Kirkpatrick approach is clear: showing the results of each step provides a very compelling argument that the T&D program was valuable and produced a positive business impact.

The problem is that this model puts business impact at the end of the evaluation, following two difficult measurement steps. It usually is not practical, and sometimes not even feasible, to demonstrate that specific learning occurred and that it is being applied on the job. As a result, business impact often is never measured or demonstrated. A Strategic Analytics approach focuses more on the ultimate intent, putting business impact front and center in the diagnostic.

Training alone or as part of a larger set of changes? Recall the discussion in chapter 1 about measuring the impact of HR programs. Evaluating T&D programs is a classic case. T&D programs usually are a number of steps removed from any clear and direct impact on business outcomes, so it is very difficult to establish that link. Because T&D programs are typically developed in response to perceived competency gaps, the canonical approach to measuring their success focuses on closing those competency gaps. The program is deemed successful if it can be shown that the gap was closed.

As attractive as this conclusion might be, the problem lies in the assumption that the T&D program alone is the right intervention in the first place. A competency gap can be shown for virtually every role in an organization. Whenever roles are considered in a vacuum, it is very easy to argue that competencies always should be improved. Roles are never perfectly designed and staffed, nor are current T&D approaches ever ideal. Thus a narrow focus only on competency gaps will almost always come to the conclusion that important improvements can be made.

A broader view considers the other deficiencies in organizational design, aside from imperfectly designed roles and responsibilities. Compensation is a blunt tool: it is not well suited for motivating the right behavior in most roles. Feedback and information sharing almost always fall short of what is needed to support high performance. Accountability for performance always can be improved. The level of cross-functional collaboration rarely is what the strategy requires. Leaders get distracted and cannot focus on everything that matters precisely when their focused attention is most needed. And so on.

T&D is only one of a large number of interventions that may be able to improve organizational effectiveness. The Strategic Analytics approach includes considering non-T&D interventions either in conjunction with or instead of T&D. This casts a much wider net than the Kirkpatrick approach, which focuses only on the T&D intervention.

The other widely advocated approach for evaluating T&D programs is ROI (Phillips, 1994). As discussed in chapter 2, ROI is overly difficult to calculate correctly, is too focused on short-term cash flow impacts, and does not address the causal factors needed to improve organizational capability.

Common outcomes of T&D programs can include improved competencies or leadership behaviors that are identified as important for organizational effectiveness. The contributions to organizational effectiveness can include benefits such as clearer communication about goals and priorities, better feedback, more seamless cross-functional collaboration, better career planning and talent management, among others. In order for those benefits to be included in an ROI calculation they have to be translated into monetary terms.

For example, clearer communication about goals and priorities can lessen the amount of time needed to complete a work process; in turn this might be traced to more efficient use of resources and a monetary benefit that can be included in an ROI calculation. However, the benefits of better communication do not necessarily show up directly and immediately in more efficient resource use. Instead more efficient use of resources is often realized only after a significant delay following the improved communication and/or in conjunction with other interventions such as team coaching, improved leadership and IT support, changes in the work design, and others. The benefit of improved communication can be expressed in monetary terms and included in ROI only in the minority of cases where it has an immediate and direct impact on resource efficiency.

The more important issue is whether improving the capability directly contributes to improved ability to execute the strategy. This is nontrivial, because it's difficult to link individual competencies to capabilities and performance at the group or business unit level. From the example above, how does better communication about goals and priorities contribute to strategy execution and organizational effectiveness? The answer is it *can*, depending on the context and what is getting in the way of improved organizational capability; yet it also easily could be a "nice to have" improvement in leadership behaviors that does not have any material impact on strategy execution and organizational effectiveness. To assess which case is true, you need to apply Strategic Analytics.

Build versus buy versus redesign. The Strategic Analytics approach starts with considering a much larger question than the impact of a specific T&D program. The right place to start is a systems analysis of T&D relative to the costs and benefits of acquiring skills from outside the organization.

The classic question is whether it makes more sense to build or to buy the skills that you need. There are a number of reasons why developing people from within is a sound strategy. Your current employees are a match for your culture. You have seen them perform and know the kind of effort they will put in. If you don't develop your current employees, you may risk losing them.

On the other hand, there are strong arguments for hiring from outside. External hires have a proven track record. If they have already demonstrated the skills working someplace else, the chances are good that they will be able to perform in your organization even if the culture is different. Promoting people internally into a new role, in contrast, carries the uncertainty of not knowing if they will be able to perform the enhanced job duties.

This is the classic build versus buy argument. However, there is a third consideration that typically is ignored: diagnosing whether changes in the work design should be part of the decision making process. The only truly effective way to determine the answer to a build versus buy decision is to understand the entire system and how the skills contribute. Questions to be addressed should include:

- Would redesigning the work improve productivity?
- Can it be used as a substitute for or complement to building skills from within or purchasing them from outside?

Roles have many tasks, some of which are harder for most people to perform, and some of which are easier. For example, all managers have to do routine computer and calendaring tasks. Senior executives whose time is viewed as very valuable have administrative assistants assigned to them to lessen the time they spend on routine tasks. Similarly, health care organizations sometimes use scribes who accompany doctors as they see patients, to lessen the time doctors spend putting notes in medical files. In both these cases, the administrative help enables the executive or doctor to spend more work time using skills that are more expensive and harder to develop (than administrative skills).

Examining the potential benefits of redesigning the work happens all the time. The problem is that it usually is done predominantly by executives whose strengths are strategy or engineering, and who do not work directly with the people in the roles. They need to better coordinate the redesign work with HR representatives and lower-level managers who know the strengths and weaknesses of both the roles and the people working in them.

Similarly, when HR representatives or lower-level managers are faced with a role where vacancies pose perennial problems because people can't be trained quickly enough from within or hired fast enough from outside, they should consider the redesign option as part of the Strategic Analytics diagnostic. They may not have permission to carry out a redesign. But the diagnostic can reveal key deficiencies with focusing exclusively on skill building or hiring.

Focusing narrowly on efforts to build skills just because they seem like a good idea is bad HR practice. There is no guarantee of improving strategy execution and organizational effectiveness. Conducting a thorough Strategic Analytics diagnostic will reveal what the best interventions are. Though the initial knee-jerk diagnosis might have been to run a T&D program, the results could reveal that T&D is only part of the solution or perhaps not even a good choice.

Conclusion

Key Learning and Action Points

In this concluding chapter I summarize key learning points from the book, along with recommendations for diagnosing and improving strategy execution and organizational effectiveness.

Strategic Analytics is a team sport. Right now both senior leadership and HR are leaving value on the table. We have to end the "business as usual," nonintegrated way enterprise analytics and human capital analytics are conducted.

The lack of coordination is understandable at first glance. People are very busy: dividing analytics up into separate domains assigned to senior leaders and HR makes the task seem easy, especially since each group conducts the analytics it knows best. But the divide-and-conquer approach is precisely where things go wrong.

Both sides ignore critical information needed for a comprehensive diagnostic. In their annual cycle of fine-tuning the strategy and budgeting, senior leaders largely ignore the human capital perspective. They think they know the business inside and out, but they have blind spots about the drivers of employee behavior and performance. They usually incorrectly assume that any employee issue can be solved with only minor tweaks to the work design. Senior leaders are far removed from HR issues; some assume people can be easily manipulated to produce whatever performance is needed.

HR has a different set of blind spots that are just as damaging. They do not align employee behaviors and competencies with the needs of the business and strategy execution. When they focus on business-related outcomes, if at all, they often overemphasize ROI, program efficiency, and financial impacts that can be measured in money terms. They do not focus sufficiently on organization capability that supports competitive advantage.

There is a bit of a chicken-versus-egg challenge in the current situation. Unlike finance, which is deeply involved in measuring business performance, HR historically has rarely had insights it could contribute that would directly inform discussions of strategy execution. The problem is that many HR professionals are not highly analytical. HR has to embrace analytical approaches, like the one outlined in figure 16, to help the

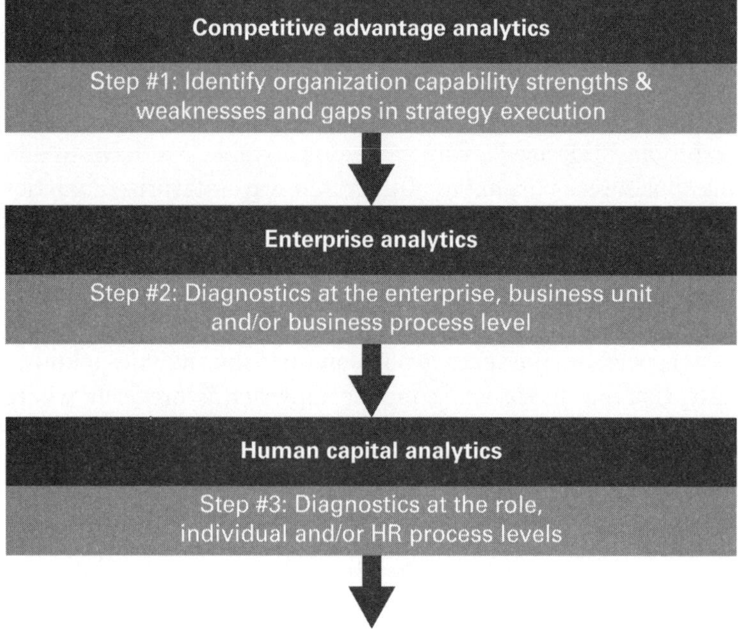

Figure 16: Strategic Analytics Roadmap

business make better decisions. People in HR have to master their part of the analysis, which requires greater analytic capability than many have today.

A core capability is building and testing causal models. This does not require multivariate statistics skills; it does, though, require the ability to work with statistical experts who can run those models if needed. HR business partners need to be able to lead analytical processes like the roadmap in figure 16.

HR is not alone in needing to change its approach to analysis and decision making. Senior business leaders share an equal responsibility to achieve better integration of HR and human capital analytics into annual budgeting and strategic decision making. Given the time needed to conduct thorough analyses, the organization needs more of an iterative process for making planning decisions throughout the year. Rather than set all budgets and strategic decisions in stone before the fiscal year starts, organizations need to conduct ongoing testing and measurement throughout the year. Mid-cycle adjustments to budget allocations and strategic priorities should be made as needed. The precise adjustments will depend on the analysis results.

This tends to happen already with very high-profile new ventures, like Boeing's 787 Dreamliner. In such cases, the company makes an ironclad commitment to figure out how to make a new business or innovation work. Everyone collectively does whatever it takes to support the new venture, including making mid-year adjustments without waiting for the next annual planning cycle. More problems typically arise with ongoing operations whenever you are trying to grow capabilities while staying within the confines of the annual budgeting cycle. In these cases, senior leaders typically make budgeting and strategic goal-setting decisions without sufficiently consulting HR.

Most enterprise and human capital processes are not managed strategically because the analytics are not integrated. Senior business leaders have to embrace the human capital analytics role HR has to play. HR has to meet the challenge by building analytics capability in its business partner ranks and, where appropriate, in centers of excellence.

Cash is king, but finance is not. The finance function emphasizes cash flow because it's tangible, and cash is king when times are tight. Yet you often need to deplete cash in the short term to build the ability to generate more cash long term.

In order to show a positive ROI, an investment simply has to have a positive cash flow. However, positive cash flow does not ensure improved execution of your strategy and may even be contrary to it. Any change that squeezes costs while keeping sales the same will show a positive ROI. In contrast, improving strategy execution usually requires investing in capability. If the investment dollars do not yield a short-term increase in revenue, then short-term ROI can be negative even if the potential for longer-term revenue increases substantially. Increasing cash flow does not have to be at odds with strategy execution. But increasing cash flow usually is not a strategic goal unless you are on the verge of bankruptcy.

Strategic Analytics can determine what parts of the organization design are more important for competitive advantage. With that information, you can determine where you can cut spending to generate additional cash without measurably degrading the very capability you need to succeed in the long run.

You can't scorecard your way to success unless analytics leads the way. The human capital metrics that populate the people quadrant of balanced scorecards today are rarely strategic. Most human capital scorecard metrics help the organization better manage expenses by focusing on efficiency of HR processes, safety, and turnover. The metrics can point the way to financial benefits through increased cash flow. However, they are usually not directly related to the organizational capabilities needed for successful strategy execution.

Safety, for example, is a common metric that is important to achieve. However, it is similar to positive cash flow: you need it to survive as an organization if times have been very rough (poor safety; hemorrhaging cash), but it is only a necessary, not a sufficient, condition for strategic success.

A Strategic Analytics diagnostic can identify metrics for your scorecards that tell you what you need to accomplish to improve strategy execution.

Focus on both your strengths and weaknesses. The causes of strategic failure and organizational ineffectiveness often grow in the space between jobs: the tasks that are no one's primary duty to complete. Processes often fall apart because no one role has sole responsibility for making sure things happen the right way. Are performance management and rewards too focused on individuals? Would there be greater accountability and would people take more responsibility if the work was managed more collectively?

Strategic Analytics helps identify inconsistencies in the organizational design that get in the way of making those improvements. What elements of the design make it easier or harder for people to do their jobs and execute the strategy? Where do shortcomings in the organization design interfere with the lateral integration and cross-functional/cross-business-unit collaboration necessary for successful strategy execution? Understanding those challenges is key to determining where systematic problems with strategy execution may arise.

Put the horse in front of the cart. Both business and HR leaders construct narratives about the way things happen in organizations by starting with individual jobs. Sales are viewed as originating from people in sales roles. Innovative breakthroughs come from R&D roles. Supply chain challenges are dealt with by people in logistics roles. And so on.

Those narratives are compelling but too simplistic. Each of those jobs has a very important role to play, but each is only one of many that together produce the desired organizational outcomes. Roles are interdependent, so effective strategy execution depends on multiple people doing aligned actions. You need to use Strategic Analytics to build a causal model and diagnose the strengths and weaknesses of the entire system. The causal model often will lead you back to specific roles once the solutions have been identified. But you have to start with the system and work your way back to the role, not the other way around.

There are a thousand things you can improve with individual roles: the people's skills, how they are managed, the communication and feedback they receive, and so on. The vast majority of those changes are "nice to have" but not central to improved strategy execution. The Strategic Analytics diagnostic helps identify what's critical and needs to be addressed first.

Correlation is not causation. Why is it that everyday decisions in board rooms and C suites are made on the basis of nothing more than correlational data? The need to make decisions too quickly forces senior leaders' hands: they have no choice but to use correlational data because that's all that's immediately available.

Prioritizing the analytics and when to conduct them is extremely important. A comprehensive application of Strategic Analytics can take some time to complete. For analytics to be relevant and useful, you need to sequence them to take place in synch with the annual strategy setting and budgeting process.

Many challenges fall into the category of "perennial problems": issues that have been recognized for some time and that keep coming up every year because they are never fully solved. Today, the vast majority of analytics in these cases is conducted at a pace that alternates between a snail crawl and a fire drill. For most of the year little (if any) progress is made on analyzing the issues because they are not an urgent priority. Then, a key stakeholder suddenly realizes that a problem has to be addressed ASAP, so the organization goes into firefighting mode. Tons of attention and resources are focused on the problem, but with unrealistic expectations for the time needed to complete rigorous analytics.

It is much better to look forward into the planning cycle, and the rhythm of the business, for the key moments in the future when people are likely to again focus their attention on the perennial problem. From there, work your way back to the current day, determine what kinds of analytics are needed to get to actionable insight, make a plan, and then launch the analysis. That way, you will be ready with the deeply-researched answers when the fire drill starts and when leaders want answers "right now!"

This is not an idle recommendation. Most work I have done that had the greatest impact has followed this format: do the analysis under the radar on a key organizational issue, so the results are ready when the issue is suddenly elevated to a high-priority status.

High performance is a work design choice, not a state of mind. High performance sometimes can be achieved in the short term through sheer will alone. If your team faces a major deadline, you can rally them to deliver high performance through communication and persuasion. However, sustained high performance is driven by the work design, not a "win one for the team" mentality.

High-performance work design is complex. To make it work, you have to design and align many different organizational parts and processes. This includes pushing decision making down to the lowest level possible, sharing critical information so frontline employees can make autonomous decisions, hiring and training employees who have the skills to make those decisions, providing compensation that supports and rewards higher productivity, and managing more through coaching and influence than micromanaging.

The multiple interrelated parts in a high-performance work system create lots of opportunities for things to go wrong. Employees may lack the information needed for optimal decision making. Rewards may not sufficiently differentiate high from low performers. Compensation may not attract the best performers. Managers may revert to micromanaging at the first sign of poor performance. And so on. You need Strategic Analytics to diagnose where to find the areas of improvement that will support sustained high performance. A piecemeal approach to analytics will not identify the right levers.

Show that the money matters. Some leaders think everyone who works for them should be paid top dollar; others have the opposite viewpoint. Neither one is correct. You need to look at each role's contribution in terms of high performance and the part it plays in building and maintaining the organizational capability that provides competitive advantage.

Roles that are part of high-performance work design typically require higher compensation relative to similar jobs in other organizations. The higher compensation is needed to attract and retain people capable of sustained high performance. Even when a role is not part of a high-performance work design, higher compensation may be warranted to keep turnover down and avoid the costs of disruption from extended vacancies.

Many jobs in organizations are important without satisfying either the high-performance criteria or contributing directly to building and maintaining competitive advantage. The argument that someone in a role should be highly paid because important work would not get done without a particular person misses the point. All roles are important at some level, or the work would be irrelevant to the products and services the organization delivers to its customers. Showing that a role or person can be important is not sufficient to justify premium pay. You have to make the additional argument for the importance of premium pay as part of the strategic contribution of the role.

Culture is not carved in stone. Culture is often viewed as an immutable aspect of organizational life, yet it can be changed. Part of what makes a culture so strong is the multiple aspects of design and capability that reinforce and support it. People who work well in the culture are more likely to get hired and promoted. People who do not are less likely to be hired and are more likely to leave. Rewards, both explicit and informal, are finely tuned to emphasize the behaviors desired by the culture, including positive feedback from leaders and peers for those behaviors. And so on.

Strategic Analytics provides a comprehensive assessment of all the parts of the organization that support and reinforce the culture. It also shows the options for changing the culture by addressing the work system, while highlighting the interconnected nature of all the different pieces. Changing culture is difficult, but doable. The Strategic Analytics diagnostic can provide a comprehensive road map for starting and completing a cultural transformation.

References

Beer, Michael (2009). *High Commitment, High Performance*, San Francisco, CA: Jossey-Bass.

Blumberg, Melvin and Charles D. Pringle (1982). "The missing opportunity in organizational research: Some implications for a theory of work performance," *Academy of Management Review*, 7(4), 560–69.

Boudreau, John W. and Peter M. Ramstad (2007). *Beyond HR: The New Science of Human Capital*, Boston, MA: Harvard Business Review Press.

Cohen, Aaron (1993). "Organizational commitment and turnover: A meta-analysis," *Academy of Management Journal*, 36(5), 1140–57.

Cropanzano, Russell, Deborah E. Rupp, and Zinta S. Byrne (2003). "The relationship of emotional exhaustion to work attitudes, job performance, and organizational citizenship behaviors," *Journal of Applied Psychology*, 88(1), 160–69.

Drucker, Peter (1967). *The Effective Executive*, New York: Harper & Row.

Galbraith, Jay R. (2009). *Designing Matrix Organizations That Actually Work*, San Francisco, CA: Jossey-Bass.

Galbraith, Jay R. (2014). *Designing Organizations: Strategy, Structure, and Process at the Business Unit and Enterprise Levels*, San Francisco, CA: Jossey-Bass.

Hackman, J. Richard and Edward E. Lawler, III (1971). "Employee reactions to job characteristics," *Journal of Applied Psychology*, 55(3), 259-86.

Harter, James K., Frank L. Schmidt, and Theodore L. Hayes (2002). "Business-unit-level relationship between employee satisfaction, employee engagement, and business outcomes: A meta-analysis," *Journal of Applied Psychology*, 87(2), 268-79.

Heskett, James L., W. Earl Sasser, and Leonard A. Schlesinger (1997). *The Service Profit Chain*, New York: The Free Press.

Kaplan, Robert S. and David P. Norton (1996). *The Balanced Scorecard: Translating Strategy into Action*. Boston, MA: Harvard Business School Press.

Kaplan, Robert S. and David P. Norton (2004). *Strategy Maps: Converting Intangible Assets into Tangible Outcomes*. Boston, MA: Harvard Business Review Press.

Kirkpatrick, Donald L. and James D. Kirkpatrick (2006). *Evaluating Training Programs: The Four Levels*, 3rd Edition, San Francisco, CA: Berrett-Koehler.

Latham, Gary P. (2007). *Work Motivation: History, Theory, Research, and Practice*, Thousand Oaks, CA: Sage Publications.

Lawler, Edward E., III (2003). *Treat People Right: How Organizations and Individuals Can Propel Each Other into a Virtuous Spiral of Success*, San Francisco, CA: Jossey-Bass.

Lawler, Edward E., III and Christopher G. Worley (2011). *Management Reset: Organizing for Sustainable Effectiveness*, San Francisco, CA: Jossey-Bass.

Levenson, Alec (2009). "Measuring and maximizing the business impact of executive coaching," *Consulting Psychology Journal: Practice and Research*, 61(2), 103–21.

Levenson, Alec (2011). "Using targeted analytics to improve talent decisions," *People & Strategy*, 34(2), 34-43.

Levenson, Alec (2014a). *Employee Surveys That Work: Improving Design, Use, and Organizational Impact*, San Francisco, CA: Berrett-Koehler.

Levenson, Alec (2014b). "Learning analytics that maximize individual and organizational performance," in E. Biech, ed., *ASTD Handbook: The Definitive Reference for Training & Development*, Second Edition, ASTD Press, 553-63.

Levenson, Alec and Tracey Faber (2009). "Using human capital measurement to drive productivity," *HR Magazine*, 68-74, June.

Levenson, Alec, Michael J. Fenlon, and George Benson (2010). "Rethinking retention strategies: Work-life versus deferred compensation in a total rewards strategy," *WorldAtWork Journal*, Fourth Quarter, 41-52.

Levenson, Alec R., Wim A. Van der Stede, and Susan G. Cohen (2006). "Measuring the relationship between managerial competencies and performance," *Journal of Management*, 32(3), 360–80.

Mohrman, Susan Albers, Susan G. Cohen, and Allan M. Mohrman, Jr. (1995). *Designing Team-Based Organizations: New Forms for Knowledge Work*, San Francisco, CA: Jossey-Bass.

Mulvey, Paul W. and Gerald Ledford (2002). Implementing reward systems. In J. W. Hedge and E. D. Pulakos, eds., *Implementing Organizational Interventions: Steps, Processes, and Best Practices*. San Francisco, CA: Jossey-Bass, 133-66.

O'Boyle, Ernest, Jr. and Herman Aguinis (2012). "The best and the rest: Revisiting the norm of normality of individual performance," *Personnel Psychology*, 65, 79–119.

Phillips, Jack (1994). *Measuring Return on Investment, Volume 1*, ASTD Press.

Porath, Christine, Gretchen M. Spreitzer, Cristina Gibson, and Flannery G. Garnett (2012). "Thriving at work: Toward its measurement, construct validation, and theoretical refinement," *Journal of Organizational Behavior*, 33(2), 250–71.

Roulston, Kathryn, Kathleen deMarrais, and Jamie B. Lewis (2003). "Learning to interview in the social sciences," *Qualitative Inquiry*, 9(4), 643–68.

Rucci, Anthony J., Steven P. Kirn, and Richard T. Quinn (1998). "The employee-customer-profit chain at Sears," *Harvard Business Review*, 76(1), January.

Taylor, Frederick (1923). *The Principles of Scientific Management*, New York: Harper and Row.

Weiss, Robert S. (1995). *Learning from Strangers: The Art and Method of Qualitative Interview Studies*. New York: The Free Press.

Worley, Christopher G., Thomas Williams, and Edward E. Lawler, III (2014). *The Agility Factor: Building Adaptable Organizations for Superior Performance*. San Francisco, CA: Jossey-Bass.

Appendix

Strategic Analytics Diagnostic Interview Template

Chapters 3 through 6 present the steps for doing a full Strategic Analytics diagnostic. This appendix provides a comprehensive template that you can use to design an interview to diagnose whatever issue you want to address in executing your strategy. The questions are drawn from those chapters.

This is not a tool you should use "as is." Instead, it provides you a template for addressing the inquiry and structuring the interviews with stakeholders. No diagnostic will use all the questions presented here. The most rigorous and comprehensive diagnostics I personally have led used only a subset.

It's best to consider the template like a buffet from which you want to create a balanced meal. The balance comes from selecting the right topics or questions from each main category. What items you select to use within each category will depend on your particular situation (and appetite).

There are seven categories in all:

1. Strategic context and causal model
2. Organization design
3. Organizational capability

4. Culture and group behaviors
5. Job design
6. Individual capability
7. Attitudes and motivation

If you do not have enough time, energy, and resources for a prolonged inquiry, you can do a more cursory analysis of the categories. In some cases that might mean spending only a few hours or at most a day on a category. But totally ignoring a category is too risky. You need to know at least the basics of what's going on within each of the seven categories—or to be able to explain convincingly why it does not apply. See the case studies in chapter 7 for examples.

1. **Strategic context and causal model**
   a. *Main things you need to know*
      i. Which organizational capabilities support your competitive advantage?
      ii. What specific improvements are needed to execute your strategy better?
      iii. What causal model explains your organization's performance? What are the more likely drivers of effective performance and execution of your strategy, and why? What roles do specific jobs and processes play in building and maintaining competitive advantage?
      iv. Where are the limits? Where will leaders be unwilling to change the organization to improve strategy execution and organizational performance?
   b. *Sample questions to address*
      i. What challenges keep your senior leaders up at night? What are your competitive advantage weaknesses where competitors can encroach?

ii. What information do you need about people and processes to diagnose the problems with strategy execution? Are you relying too much on existing data, investing too little in exploration? Which stakeholders can provide objective data and accurate assessments of the situation?

iii. How do specific roles and business processes contribute to competitive advantage?

iv. Are you trying to improve short-term cash flow, long-term competitive advantage, or both? Are you focusing too much on incremental improvements that only tweak existing operations? Are you appropriately focusing on improving strategy execution where it's most needed?

v. Are there perennial issues, that is, ones that come up repeatedly? If yes, what solutions were tried before, and how did people evaluate what happened? If no, why are you addressing the problems for the first time?

vi. Are key stakeholders aligned on the problem? Do they agree on how you make money and on what the sources of your competitive advantage are (what business you are really in)?

vii. What do people think they "know" about what's going on that is based on incomplete or erroneous data analysis?

viii. Are structural issues too hard to address and therefore downplayed? Why?

ix. Is there a burning platform for change? How can the analysis help make the case?

x. Are you trying to save money in the wrong places by cutting back on compensation where you need high performance?

xi. Are you holding people accountable for scorecard or HR metrics that don't really contribute to competitive advantage?

2. **Organization design**

   a. *Main things you need to know*

      i. In what ways does the organization design support (or undermine) the capabilities that promote your competitive advantage?

      ii. How do people overcome the flaws in the organization design?

      iii. Where do breakdowns in communication and collaboration occur?

   b. *Sample questions to address*

      i. How are decision rights allocated?

      ii. Where do problems arise in decision making? Are conflicts resolved efficiently?

      iii. Where is better collaboration needed to improve strategy execution?

      iv. Do clear accountabilities tie the team's objectives to the strategy?

      v. Are people rewarded for putting the needs of the enterprise over the narrow self-interests of their team or function?

      vi. Would reconfiguring the team to be more autonomous and self-managing increase engagement and productivity?

3. **Organizational capability**

   a. *Main things you need to know*

      i. What contribution does each role play in creating the organization's capability?

ii. Where is process excellence at odds with the need for local adaptability?

iii. Are resources properly allocated to support the strategy?

iv. What are the interdependencies among the roles? How important is group collaboration and performance versus individual job performance?

b. *Sample questions to address*

i. For any given role, how much is contributing to competitive advantage a core part of the job versus a sideline activity?

ii. How do people in support functions prioritize their tasks and services for particular teams?

iii. How can the boundaries between the team's responsibilities and the responsibilities of other teams, functions, and business units be better defined and managed?

iv. If teams complain about restrictive processes, do they have the enterprise's strategic objectives in mind, or do they just want to ease their burden?

v. How can the compensation for a team or role be better aligned with its productivity and quality goals?

vi. Are you focusing on areas where making a change would make a difference? Are you focusing too much on a role's average contribution rather than on room for (marginal) improvement?

vii. Does the team operate as a well-integrated group or a collection of individuals?

4. **Culture and group behaviors**

   a. *Main things you need to know*

      i. Where does culture enhance (or impede) strategy execution?

      ii. What behaviors does the organization's culture encourage and support? Are they consistent with strategy execution and organizational effectiveness?

      iii. How does the organization design, including rewards, reinforce the culture?

      iv. Do teams operate effectively to accomplish their goals?

   b. *Sample questions to address*

      i. Where is the culture strong or weak?

      ii. What cultural elements are needed for the most effective strategy execution?

      iii. What types of behaviors do the performance management and rewards systems explicitly encourage?

      iv. Do the members of a group collectively have the responsibility, skills, motivation, coordination, and support needed to accomplish the group's objectives?

      v. Do you focus too much on the individual and not enough on group performance and dynamics?

      vi. Are team members aligned on what they are supposed to accomplish and the methods for doing so (shared understanding)?

      vii. Are the team's goals set appropriately?

      viii. Do the team members trust and support each other in getting their work done?

ix. Do they proactively share information with each other?

x. Are the members committed to the team?

xi. Is the team collectively held accountable for its performance?

xii. Are the team's actions focused on producing the operational outcomes needed for successful strategy execution?

5. **Job design**

   a. *Main things you need to know*

      i. Is the job design consistent with the performance expectations?

      ii. Could greater productivity be achieved if the job were enriched or enlarged?

      iii. How interdependent is the job on other roles on the team and (more broadly) in the organization?

   b. *Sample questions to address*

      i. Are the performance expectations consistent with the compensation for each role?

      ii. Could your current employees perform an enriched job with additional training and experience, or would they have to be replaced?

      iii. Could current employees handle the work load if the job were enlarged?

      iv. Are there gaps in accountability at the individual role level because of the interdependencies at the group level?

      v. Given all the different objectives assigned to a job, do the people in the role prioritize correctly to perform all critical tasks?

vi. Do the supervisors have the competencies needed to coach, cajole, and/or command their employees to perform in line with the strategic priorities?

6. **Individual capability**

   a. *Main things you need to know*

      i. Do the capabilities of current employees match job design requirements?

      ii. What is the cost of developing the competencies from within versus hiring from outside?

      iii. Which competencies can be more readily learned through training and which through on-the-job experience?

   b. *Sample questions to address*

      i. Which competencies are most important for improving strategy execution?

      ii. Can most of the competency gaps among current employees be closed through training and/or on-the-job experience?

      iii. Is there a ready supply of external hires that can fill the competency gaps?

      iv. Is compensation sufficient to attract and retain the right people?

      v. Is it cheaper to develop from within, even if it takes longer to close the competency gaps?

      vi. What is the variance in performance across current employees in the role?

      vii. How do the job demands compare to those of alternative jobs in the local labor market?

viii. Has the benchmark for external compensation risen faster than, slower than, or on par with inflation?

ix. Could organizational capability be maintained with slightly cheaper talent or increased with the same price talent?

7. **Attitudes and motivation**

a. *Main things you need to know*

i. Are people motivated to perform at the levels required by the design?

ii. What parts of the job and organization attract people to work for you and keep them from leaving?

iii. What makes them committed and willing to go the extra mile?

b. *Sample questions to address*

i. What are the drivers of job satisfaction and thriving on the job?

ii. How do supervisors support (or fail to support) their employees?

iii. What do employees want in terms of career development and opportunities for advancement?

iv. Is the workload too high for the compensation?

v. Do the employees have work-life balance, or are they burning out?

vi. How could goal setting be improved?

vii. Are people held accountable for their performance?

Acknowledgments

I owe deep thanks to each of the following people. David Berke, Jennifer Deal, and Chris Worley for providing feedback at key points in the development of the book. Lacey Leone McLaughlin and Anjelica Garcia for helping to launch me on the path of converting tacit knowledge into something accessible to others. The business and HR executives and practitioners with whom I have had the privilege and honor to work over the years; our work together is the foundation on which this entire book is based. The list includes, but is not limited to, Tracy Faber, Patrick McLaughlin, Kim Warmbier, Jeff Joerres, Tony Sarsam, Husodo Angkosubroto, Terry Hueneke, Anne Sutanto, Wenwu Xiang, Anne Donovan, Mike Fenlon, Bianca Martorella, Scott Stevenson, Anne Fithern, Per Scott, Jane Dobie, Terri-Lee Weeks, Rob Carlyle, Rick Yacknovets, Samantha Rees, Brendan Howard, Michael Johnson, Steve Campbell, Meghan Henson, Inge Zhang, Bernard Bedon, James Taylor, Val Kroenke, Samantha Wasserman, Rebekka Gordon, Tom Leitko, Sharon Jacobson, Mike McDermott, Joe Bonito, Tim Hickey, Sam Amelio, Jennifer Boyd, Bob Bowen, Eric Ingram, Alan May, Jose Motta, Ben Nemo, Jackson Lynch,

Julie Bohannen Nanney, David Harris, David Oliver, Lauren McEntire, Allison Baker, Dee Alcott-Rodriguez, Joe Bonito, Mike McDermott, Mark Poklar, and Mary Wayne Bush. A special thank you goes to Nancy Jagmin for providing the initial opportunities that ultimately led to numerous case studies that contributed to the book.

Index

Note: an *f* indicates a figure; an *n* indicates a note; a *t* indicates a table.

Q

R

S

About the Author

Dr. Levenson is Senior Research Scientist at the Center for Effective Organizations in the Marshall School of Business, University of Southern California. His action research and consulting with companies optimize job and organization performance and HR systems through the application of organization design, job design, human capital analytics, and strategic talent management.

Alec's work with companies combines the best elements of scientific research and practical, actionable knowledge that companies can use to improve performance. He draws from the disciplines of economics, strategy, organization behavior, and industrial-organizational psychology to tackle complex talent and organizational challenges that defy easy solutions. His recommendations focus on the actions that organizations should take to make lasting improvements in critical areas.

Alec has spent over a decade and a half training human resource professionals and teams in the application of human capital analytics across a broad range of Fortune 500 and Global 500 companies.

His research has been published in numerous academic and business publications and featured in major media outlets including *New York Times, Wall Street Journal, The Economist, CNN, Associated Press, CBS, U.S. News and World Report, National Public Radio, USA Today, Marketplace,* and *Fox News.* He received his PhD and MA in Economics from Princeton University and his BA in Economics and Chinese language (double major) from the University of Wisconsin-Madison.

Berrett-Koehler is an independent publisher dedicated to an ambitious mission: *connecting people and ideas to create a world that works for all.*

We believe that to truly create a better world, action is needed at all levels—individual, organizational, and societal. At the individual level, our publications help people align their lives with their values and with their aspirations for a better world. At the organizational level, our publications promote progressive leadership and management practices, socially responsible approaches to business, and humane and effective organizations. At the societal level, our publications advance social and economic justice, shared prosperity, sustainability, and new solutions to national and global issues.

A major theme of our publications is "Opening Up New Space." Berrett-Koehler titles challenge conventional thinking, introduce new ideas, and foster positive change. Their common quest is changing the underlying beliefs, mindsets, institutions, and structures that keep generating the same cycles of problems, no matter who our leaders are or what improvement programs we adopt.

We strive to practice what we preach—to operate our publishing company in line with the ideas in our books. At the core of our approach is stewardship, which we define as a deep sense of responsibility to administer the company for the benefit of all of our "stakeholder" groups: authors, customers, employees, investors, service providers, and the communities and environment around us.

We are grateful to the thousands of readers, authors, and other friends of the company who consider themselves to be part of the "BK Community." We hope that you, too, will join us in our mission.

A BK Business Book

This book is part of our BK Business series. BK Business titles pioneer new and progressive leadership and management practices in all types of public, private, and nonprofit organizations. They promote socially responsible approaches to business, innovative organizational change methods, and more humane and effective organizations.

Connecting people and ideas
to create a world that works for all

Dear Reader,

Thank you for picking up this book and joining our worldwide community of Berrett-Koehler readers. We share ideas that bring positive change into people's lives, organizations, and society.

To welcome you, we'd like to offer you a free e-book. You can pick from among twelve of our bestselling books by entering the promotional code **BKP92E** here: http://www.bkconnection.com/welcome.

When you claim your free e-book, we'll also send you a copy of our e-newsletter, the *BK Communiqué*. Although you're free to unsubscribe, there are many benefits to sticking around. In every issue of our newsletter you'll find

- A free e-book
- Tips from famous authors
- Discounts on spotlight titles
- Hilarious insider publishing news
- A chance to win a prize for answering a riddle

Best of all, our readers tell us, "Your newsletter is the only one I actually read." So claim your gift today, and please stay in touch!

Sincerely,

Charlotte Ashlock
Steward of the BK Website

Questions? Comments? Contact me at bkcommunity@bkpub.com.